The making of

THE
STONE
ROSES

The making of
THE STONE ROSES

Nigel Cawthorne

"My son Colin Cawthorne researched this book, produced a first draft and collaborated in producing the final manuscript. He is essentially the co-author of 'The Making of The Stone Roses.'"
Nigel Cawthorne, London, 2005

The publisher wishes to thank the Book Division at Lasgo Chrysalis London for their ongoing support in developing this series.

Published by Unanimous Ltd.
Unanimous Ltd. is an imprint of MQ Publications Ltd.
12 The Ivories, 6–8 Northampton Street, London, N1 2HY

Printed and bound in France

ISBN: 1 90331 878 5

1 2 3 4 5 6 7 8 9

Picture credits:
Cover: © Kevin Cummins/Idols.
Picture section: page 97 © Michel Linssen/Redferns; pages 98–99 and page 100 (top) © Ian Tilton/Retna; page 100 (bottom) and page 101 (top) © Paul Slattery/Retna; page 101 (bottom) © City Life, Manchester, www.citylife.co.uk; page 102 (top) © Ian Tilton/Retna; page 102 (bottom) © Ged Murray/Rex Features; page 103 (both) © Ian Tilton/Retna; page 104 © Brian Rasic/Rex Features

contents

introduction

In April 1989 The Stone Roses released their debut album, the eponymous *The Stone Roses*. It was heralded as the defining record of the decade and showered with critical praise. Although *The Stone Roses* posed as an effortless fusion of dance and rock, it was the product of five years of toil. The album itself charts the development of the band over that period and the titles of its tracks provide the chapter headings of *The Making of The Stone Roses*.

Singer Ian Brown, guitarist John Squire, bassist Andy Couzens, and drummer Alan Wren (a.k.a. Reni) got together in Manchester, England in the early 1980s to form the post-punk street band The Stone Roses. They struggled to make a name for themselves in the burgeoning "Madchester" scene. Then on October 23, 1984 Pete Townshend of The Who held an anti-heroin benefit at the Moonlight Club in Hampstead, North London where The Stone Roses first came to the attention of a wider audience. At the end of the evening Townshend played a couple of tracks with them, endorsing the talent of the up-and-coming band.

The Stone Roses went back to Manchester and played the local circuit. They wrote their songs and honed their unique sound under railroad arches and in disused industrial buildings. Their early gigs were at the city's infamous "warehouse parties"—a precursor of the underground rave scene. Soon they earned themselves the reputation of being one of the best live acts in Manchester, then the whole of the UK.

As the tracks for the album evolved, the band went through a number of management changes. One altercation led to the replacement of Andy Couzens with Gary Mountfield (a.k.a. Mani). As a result, various tracks came out as singles on competing record labels. However, when *The Stone Roses* album was released on Silvertone it quickly gained both critical and popular success. *The Stone Roses* was seen to capture the very essence of the time. Its fresh approach went on to revolutionize British pop. Although the band was seen internationally as icons of the Manchester scene they were never really part of it. Now the era of Madchester is over, *The Stone Roses* endures as the one of the greatest albums of all time, but it left the band creatively drained.

Producing a follow-up album was never going to be an easy task. Continuing management problems, legal difficulties, and internal bickering meant the band began to fall apart. However, in December 1994 they released *The Second Coming* to mixed reviews. In the spring of 1995, Reni left the band and was replaced by Rebel MC's Robbie Maddix, and the band set off on their one and only US tour. But The Stone Roses had already lost their magic. They soon disintegrated without fulfilling the creative promise of *The Stone Roses*.

Even so The Stone Roses leave behind an indelible legacy and a phenomenal record that still influences music on both sides of the Atlantic today.

british graffiti

The story of *The Stone Roses*, the album, is the story of The Stone Roses, the band. It chronicles the evolution of the band in the wild world of Manchester in the late 1970s and 1980s, and the upbringing and influences of the band members. Although on the surface *The Stone Roses* is an album of the dance-rock fusion that became known at Britpop, underneath it is pure punk. It was vividly illustrated by an incident when the album came out. Although many of the critics and record-buying public were raving, the band did not bask in their new-found glory. Instead they took a trip down the M6 motorway from their home in the thriving city of Manchester to the decayed industrial town of Wolverhampton 60 miles to the south.

In fact, they were supposed to be on their way to Rockfield Studios in Wales where they were to record their new single, but they had some business to attend to on the way. Before they left Manchester, they had met for a band meeting in the International club, which was the home of the new music and their base of operations. It was owned by their manager Gareth Evans. He had informed them that an old record label of theirs, FM Revolver, had just re-released their old single "Sally Cinnamon" hoping to cash in on The Stone Roses' new-found success. The band had not sanctioned this re-release and knew nothing about it until then.

They were upset as "Sally Cinnamon" was a throw-away pop track and did not represent their new more profound sound. In fact, it detracted from the break-through they had made with *The Stone Roses*. FM Revolver's chief executive Paul Birch had even had the audacity to put out a promotional video to accompany this unofficial release. At the meeting at the International, Gareth Evans showed the band the bootleg tape on the video player in his office. They watched dumbstruck, outraged at this unsanctioned portrayal of themselves and their music.

"The video was insulting," said Stone Roses' lead singer Ian Brown. "There were blokes selling fruit, a few pigeons, some black woman holding a baby, a picture of me on the front of *The Face*, a few people in flares."

This was not the image they were now seeking to project.

The Face was a youth magazine that had flourished in the UK during the early 1980s when a new wave of interest in Mod culture had emerged. A "face" is Mod-speak for a leading or influential Mod. What's more, *The Face* had recently trashed the album and the band. Mod itself was the music and fashion movement in Britain in the early 1960s that had been embraced by the Beatles, the Kinks, and the early Rolling Stones—but was perhaps personified by the Small Faces and The Who. Although The Stone Roses had ridden to prominence at the time of the revival in Mod culture, *The Stone Roses* album was seen to be a development of, or deviation from, the pure tenets of Mod—hence the trashing in *The Face*.

But what London-based journalists at *The Face* said about *The Stone Roses* was neither here nor there. What did concern the band was that a Midlands-based record company was ripping them off, with potentially devastating consequences for their future. The Stone Roses were not going to take this lying down. The members were punks who believed in direct action and decided that revenge was a dish best served hot. So they jumped in the band's truck and headed for the offices of FM Revolver, which Paul Birch ran from his large private house in the suburbs of Wolverhampton.

To reach Wolverhampton took an hour-and-a-half down the motorway, but the band members were still seething when they reached Birch's opulent suburban home. The Stone Roses had already established a reputation for their spray-paint graffiti. Early in their career they had used a graffiti campaign around Manchester to draw attention to the band. *The Stone Roses'* album cover features abstract expressionism in the style of Jackson Pollock's "action" paintings of the 1940s and 1950s. The publicity shots for the album show the band members covered in paint. And their guitars and drum kit were also splashed with paint. It was their style. So it was not surprising that they were carrying cans of paint as they walked up Paul Birch's driveway.

The Stone Roses' drummer, Alan Wren (a.k.a. Reni) rang the bell and Birch's girlfriend Olivia Darling answered the door. The band pushed their way in, demanding to see Birch. They found their way into his office but Birch insisted that, as they had not made an appointment, he would not talk to them. This was the final straw. They removed the lids from their paint cans and covered him in blue and white emulsion paint. Even Olivia Darling did not escape a little redecorating. The band then trashed Birch's office, covering everything with paint.

The Stone Roses' lead guitarist, John Squire, claimed responsibility for the incident.

"It was my idea to do it," he said, "but we didn't get very far before we got stopped. They answered the front door of the office and Reni got in first, then the rest of us and we just started chucking paint around, but they locked the door into the rest of the building and called the police."

Lead singer, Ian Brown, reckoned that Paul Birch had written a press release about the incident before the police even arrived. The next day Birch tried to sell his paint-splattered shoes as pop memorabilia.

"We told him we weren't happy with the video," said Ian Brown, who was particularly contemptuous of Birch and his attitude to music and the band. "He thinks he's got some sort of immunity because he's in the biz. He thinks we're not real people, we're just fucking puppets, performing monkeys that he can earn a buck off. He told us to make an appointment and that's when it kicked off. He's earning a lot of money off us and he tells us to make an appointment. So then we painted him. And his office and his motor—full tins."

When the cans of regular house paint were empty, they left the building. But Reni still had some aerosol cans of spray paint. So they set about a radical respray of Birch's brand new $40,000 Mercedes and two other cars in the driveway. The angry man of the band, confrontational front man, Ian Brown, finished off their vandalous handiwork by hurling a brick through the limo's rear-window.

The band were long gone before the police turned up, but were later arrested during the recording session in Wales. Ian Brown, John Squires, and Reni were picked up in their hotel in Monmouth. The bass player Gary Mountfield (a.k.a. Mani) and promoter Steve Atherton, the Adge, gave themselves up at the local police station. They were charged with criminal damage. Their subsequent court appearance did nothing to harm the sales of *The Stone Roses*. In fact, it gave them a special status in the new music that was coming out of the UK in the late 1980s. Long before the fighting Gallagher brothers of Oasis were making a name for troublemaking, The Stone Roses were the bad boys of Britpop.

i wanna be adored

The strength of *The Stone Roses* comes from the individual members of the band, who each contribute to its unique sound. In the album, lyricist Ian Brown depicts what it was like to grow up in Manchester—a once-great industrial center in northern England, which was experiencing the crisis of deindustrialization that faced many cities in the UK and north America in the 1970s and 1980s.

Though *The Stone Roses* is quintessentially a Manchester album, Ian Brown was not born there. He was born on February 23, 1963 in Warrington, a sprawling town midway between the cities of Liverpool and Manchester and part of the industrial conurbation of north-west England. He spent his early life there and fondly recalled his early childhood in the north.

"I grew up in Warrington which was grim but fun," he said. "We were poor, down to earth. My father was a joiner. He looks like me."

He had a younger brother and sister.

When Ian Brown was six years old he moved with his family to Timperley, a leafy suburb of Manchester. In 1969, they moved into Sylvan Avenue, which had been the childhood home of the Gibb brothers who went on to become the Bee Gees after the family moved to Brisbane, Australia. Two doors away lived a quiet young lad by the name of John Squire. Their friendship was to be the foundation of The Stone Roses.

Legend has it that the two met in a sandpit as toddlers soon after Brown moved to Timperley.

"There was a sandpit in the fields near our house," said Brown. "John remembers me being naked, but I don't know if that's right. I do recall the sandpit. I used to muck around in there a lot. I remember meeting John probably quite a few times, but we weren't like dead close, because I had my own mates from school. But I do recall his shy stare, which was quite intriguing even then. There was something about him."

Squire's recollection was different.

"We lived in the same street in Chorlton," he said (Chorlton-cum-Hardy is the district that embraces Timperley). "I met Ian when we were four or five in a sandpit. I was a bit dubious about him, because the lad he was playing with was bollock naked."

This meeting had a mythical quality to it—much like the meeting of The Rolling Stones' Mick Jagger and Keith Richards, who were said to have met in a sandpit as toddlers before they teamed up again as teenagers. Unlike Jagger and Richards, Brown and Squire did not go to the same elementary (primary) schools, even though they lived in the same street. The line dividing the two schools' catchment areas ran between their two houses.

"Ian was on one side and I was on the other," said Squire, "but eventually we went to the same secondary [high] school."

Brown's elementary school days were boisterous. He was immediately identified as a bright young lad, but he used his intelligence to instigate trouble.

"My first memory is being about five, at school, and being asked to give out the school milk," he recalled. "And I refused to do it. I said, 'No, just put the milk crate on the desk.

Everybody can get their own.' I think it was the first day and I thought that if I did it then, I'd have to do it every day. In the end, that's what they did, they put the milk on the desk and everyone had to come and get their own. Yeah, I changed the system. From the start you have to."

The provision of milk in British schools soon became a matter of political controversy. The UK's "Reaganite" prime minister of the 1980s, Margaret Thatcher, first came to national prominence when, as secretary of state for education and science in the 1970–74 Conservative government, she stopped the funding of milk in schools, earning herself the sobriquet ,"Thatcher, Milk Snatcher." At five, Ian Brown was already ahead of his time.

Brown's rebellious nature became the cornerstone of his appeal, both as a songwriter and a performer. In elementary (primary) school he would stand on the desks at the front of the class and do impressions of the various teachers. When chastised, he would be full of back-chat. In the playground he was the ringleader, full of charisma, charm, and a thirst for attention. It was plain that, among this contemporaries, if not the teachers, he wanted to be adored.

"A lot of teachers were wary of me, 'cos I was always quick to answer back," said Brown. "Not that I was particularly naughty, but I did have an attitude. I have never liked people telling me what to do."

As time went on, he became so unruly that he was close to being expelled from school. But then he began to put all his rebellious energy into boxing in an attempt to emulate his childhood idol Muhammad Ali, who was extremely popular in the UK at the time.

"When I was a kid, there was no bigger hero for me than Muhammad Ali," he recalled. "I can see that 1974 Foreman fight [in my mind's eye] as clear as a bell, and I got all the books. My walls were covered in Ali pictures."

It was not just the physical prowess of Muhammad Ali that the young Ian Brown aspired to. It was everything about the man. Brown admired the fact that Ali had risen to world fame from modest beginnings, overcoming all manner of social disadvantage on the way. He also admired Ali's stand against racism—which Brown abhors—and his radical political views. Ali's charisma, his insolence, his wordplay, his ruthless determination, his unshakeable self-confidence, and his justifiable arrogance were all things that Brown saw in himself, and would later try to express in his music.

Brown later went on to revere Bruce Lee and consequently made the switch from boxing to martial arts. He took this far more seriously than his boxing. It was not just another pastime for him, a way to let off some steam. His interest in martial arts verged on obsession. For seven years, he practiced karate every day after school. His ambition was to earn a black belt in the UK, then go to Japan and attain even higher grades.

After graduating from elementary school, at the age of 11, he moved to Altrincham Grammar School. This was the high school where he hooked up with John Squire again. But before he got into making music, he cycled four miles from school to the dojo (practise hall) each day. He clawed his way up through the various grades all the way up to brown belt and was just one month shy of reaching black belt when his rebellious nature took over again and he decided to pack it in.

"I still regret that I finally fell out with the discipline," he said. "I remember this kid, who was just fantastic, easily the best in the class. He was just awesome, but he had his own mind. He never took 'O' levels" (graduation exams from junior high) "and he just wouldn't do his karate the way they told him. I sort of fell into that way of thinking as well. A bit of the punk thing, I think." After their initial exposure to the New York band The Ramones, when they toured the UK in 1976, the Brits had taken punk to heart. "That kid never got beyond white belt. I think I took some of his attitude off him, which is why I eventually left the club. But I do regret it. It was a stupid thing to do."

However, the single-minded determination that Brown had learnt during his years studying karate would serve him well later on. His compulsion to reach the top would surface again when his ambition turned to music.

Music had been a growing interest in Ian Brown's life since the family had moved to Manchester. As a child he would listen to anything and everything.

"I would have been seven or eight and I had a little Dansette [portable record player]," he said later, "and my auntie gave me a pile of seven-inch singles: 'I Feel Fine' and 'Help!' by the Beatles; 'Get Off My Cloud,' 'Under My Thumb,' and 'Satisfaction' by the Rolling Stones; 'Love Child' and 'The Happening' by The Supremes, and 'It's Not Unusual' by Tom Jones. They were the first discs I had. I've still got them."

In the track "Going Down" on the *Turns Into Stone* album, he uses the line: "Her Dansette crackles to Jimi's tune." The spelling of the written lyrics indicated that this is Jimi Hendrix, who would later become one of John Squire's guitar heroes.

The first record Ian Brown bought was "Metal Guru" by T Rex. Early on, his tastes were eclectic to say the least. But then something happened that would focus his musical tastes and make music a much larger part of his life.

"Punk changed everything," he said. "The band I got into the most was the Sex Pistols. My mate had 'Anarchy In The UK.' He got it in Woollies for 29p [45 cents] because after that *Bill Grundy Show*, they put the record in the bargain bin."

The Sex Pistols had been formed by brash young entrepreneur Malcolm McLaren, who ran the "anti-fashion" boutique, named Sex, in London's Kings Road (a pivotal area of the "Swinging '60s" London scene) with now famous fashion designer, Vivienne Westwood. He felt that the overblown progressive rock at the time was out of touch with the new generation of youngsters. In early 1975, McLaren briefly managed the glitter band The New York Dolls, who became a trashy precursor of punk. Both The New York Dolls and The Ramones—the first band to embrace punk—visited the UK in the mid-1970s. In their wake, a legion of home-grown UK punk bands sprung up who, in turn, would be crucial in the development of The Stone Roses.

McLaren formed the Sex Pistols around bassist Glen Matlock, a part-time employee of Sex, with drummer Paul Cook and guitarist Steve Jones. They were looking for a singer and McLaren approached John Lydon who he had seen hanging around the jukebox in Sex. Famed for his lack of personal hygiene, particularly his green and cavity-filled teeth, Lydon was immediately dubbed Johnny Rotten.

They played their first gig on November 6, 1975 in a suburban art school. After ten minutes, the school authorities pulled the plug on them. This gave them instant standing in the nascent UK punk movement. McLaren skillfully organized publicity for the Pistols by word of mouth. Their gigs inspired the formation of other punk bands, particularly The Buzzcocks, X-Ray Specs, and The Clash.

The Buzzcocks were formed in 1975, in Manchester. The band consisted of vocalist/songwriter Howard Devoto, Pete Shelley lead guitarist, who also sang, bassist Steve Diggles and John Maher on drums. The four members met while they attended Manchester University, though, like The Stone Roses, they played the London club circuit more than Manchester. Howard Devoto left the band in 1977, to form Magazine, leaving Pete Shelley to take over leadership duties. The band toured the US twice and developed a small following there. They never achieved any significant record sales, and disbanded in the early 1980s after Pete Shelley left.

Another band around at the time, The Fall, was formed in 1976 by Mark Smith. Its first lineup was Smith (vocals, tapes, violin, keyboards), Martin Bramah (guitar), Tony Friel (bass), Una Baines (keyboards) and Karl Burns (drums). Since then they have appeared in various forms. In a recent interview, Smith said the band had had 49 members and produced 78 albums and 41 singles. They proved themselves in the run-down dancehalls of northern England's new wave scene, sometimes drawing violent reactions from hardcore fans of uncomplicated punk guitar thrash. Their debut album *Live at the Witch Trials* "served up a caustic mix of belligerently provincial urban paranoia and scorn for cultural norms, atop a deceptively unsophisticated musical arrangement".

In the summer of 1976, the Sex Pistols were being widely condemned in the press. They signed with EMI for £40,000 ($60,000) and their first single, "Anarchy In The UK," was released in December. It was backed with the often underrated "I Wanna Be Me."

As part of the publicity for the single, the band appeared on a daytime TV show. During an interview with veteran presenter Bill Grundy, they repeatedly used the word "fucker." Losing control of the interview, Grundy invited them to do their worst. They responded with a foul-mouth tirade. In the resulting furore, rock venues canceled their gigs. EMI dropped the band. Bill Grundy was fired. "Anarchy In The UK" stalled at number 38 in the UK charts and found its way into the bargain bin at Woolworths.

"I loved 'I Wanna Be Me' on the other side—that lyric about 'cover me in margarine ...' was great," Brown said. "Then I got 'God Save The Queen' the day it came out. I was 14. I remember thinking, Oh wow, that Pistols' record is gonna change the world. And it did in a way."

In March 1977, Glen Matlock left the band and was replaced by John Ritchie, who became known at Sid Vicious for his surly stance. The band was picked up for £150,000 ($225,000) by A&M Records, who promptly fired them the next week with a £75,000 ($112,500) payoff. In May, they were picked up by Richard Branson at Virgin and released "God Save The Queen"—a vicious anti-monarchy anthem whose sleeve featured Queen Elizabeth II with a safety pin through her lips. It was released to coincide with the Queen's Silver Jubilee that June. Viewed as practically treasonous, the song was banned from airplay in the UK. Consequently, it shot up the charts. The official chart merely showed a blank at number two. But independent charts put "God Save The Queen" at number one. That year, The Sex Pistols played twice in Manchester where they influenced local groups including a "boot boy" (skinhead) band called Slaughter And The Dogs, who became an important influence in the development of The Stone Roses.

Around that time, Ian Brown turned his new high school friend, John Squire, on to punk. Brown recalled how they met up again a few years after they had both moved on to Altrincham Grammar School.

"We became friendly at 13 or 14," said Brown. "When we were put into the same class at secondary school, I started chatting to him."

But when it came to music, John Squire was already streets ahead.

"He got his guitar when he was 15," Brown said. "The first thing he learned to play was 'Three Blind Mice.' Then he'd play his guitar for me when I went round."

Spending a lot of time together at a critical time in their adolescence gave them a special bond which would make them the mainstay of the band.

"He's a funny kid," said Brown. "I know he's really, really quiet and doesn't speak to no one, but when he was with me he'd never shut up. Everybody knows him as a man of few words, but in them days he was garrulous with me, definitely. I did spend a lot of my life and a lot of the Roses' life talking for the kid. I knew him so well that I'd finish his sentences off."

Brown recalled: "He was into the Beach Boys and the Beatles and didn't have any proper LPs, just compilations—

that one with the surfer on the front and the Beatles' *Live At The Hollywood Bowl*. I took around the 'God Save the Queen', first Clash LP, and 'One Chord Wonders' by the Adverts and turned him on to punk rock. After playing him these punk records, a week later he'd brought The Clash and 'God Save...' He went mad about The Clash after that, following them all over."

The Clash were a key influence on The Stone Roses. They were one of the numerous London punk bands whose formation was inspired by the Sex Pistols. Art school student, Paul Simonon, had never played an instrument before he heard the Pistols. He bought a bass and joined the band London SS with Mick Jones and Terry Chimes (a.k.a. Tory Crimes). Members of the British Conservative Party are loosely known as Tories and punk bands became an important mouthpiece for disaffected youth when the Conservative Party under Margaret Thatcher came to power in the UK in 1979.

The band's front man was John Mellor, the son of a British diplomat, who became known as Joe Strummer for his rendition, on a ukulele, of the Chuck Berry classic, "Johnny B. Goode." Mellor was an itinerant busker on the streets of London. He was also in a pub-rock band called The 101'ers (named after the torture room in George Orwell's dystopian novel *1984*) when he heard the Sex Pistols. He quit and joined Simonon, Jones, Chimes, and Keith Levene—who later left to join Public Image Ltd with Johnny Rotten after the Sex Pistols broke up—in a new band Jones called, The Clash. Their first gigs were opening for the Sex Pistols and they also toured with the Pistols on their "Anarchy in the UK" tour in 1977.

Once Brown and Squire were at the same high school, they became close friends and they spent a lot of time in each other's homes, listening to the new punk music. On a personal level though, they were chalk and cheese.

"We were total opposites," recalled Brown. "I was very outgoing, the kid that would stand on the table in front of the class doing impressions of the teachers. I was the class joker and he was the loner. He got out of sports so he could do art."

However, there was a rebellious streak in Squire too.

"I think he was the first kid in the school to play truant," said Brown, "and he did that by himself. But at 13 and 14, we'd walk the streets together and sit in each other's bedrooms playing records."

Born on November 24, 1962, John Squire was three months older than Ian Brown and was a Mancunian born and bred. As Squire pointed out: "My dad worked at GEC in Trafford Park as an electrical engineer and my mum worked in a chemist, a travel agents, a fancy goods shop, a pub. My dad gave me things he'd made, radios and stuff, and he'd pop the circuit diagram in the box just in case I needed it ... I think he harbored some sort of notion that I'd get into it one day."

But Squire's father's workplace was another victim of the deindustrialization that was taking place at the time and feeding the disillusionment of youth.

"They knocked his factory down so I'm glad I didn't follow him," said Squire. "I'm sure he wouldn't have recommended it, either. He worked there from age 14 to 65 and when he left he had the option of a carriage clock or £200. Bunch of c**ts."

Squire's family was already living in Sylvan Avenue when he was born and consequently he spent his entire childhood in Timperley. After the sandpit incident, although they did not attend the same elementary school, Squire remained conscious of Brown's presence in the area.

As Squire recalled: "I have vague memories of meeting him at his friend's house: it was like an arranged marriage, a parental thing."

At school, Squire excelled at art and, at Altrincham Grammar School, he even managed to convince his teachers to let him off sports so that he could take extra art classes; his talent was so obvious. Art—then later music—became the way that a quiet, withdrawn boy could express his air of disillusionment with authority that was so prevalent at the time.

"I was good at art," said Squire. "I drew cartoons of the teachers. There was this attitude that it didn't matter. The art teacher had that Bohemian 'I can't get the funds so why should I bother attitude' and the class saw art as time off. We only studied for two years. I ended up dropping games so I could do more."

While others around him became apathetic, Squire held on to his artistic ambition: "I always had drive," he acknowledged.

Unlike Ian Brown, Squire made few friends at school, preferring his own company. Contemporaries remember him as being quiet and shy, content to be a daydreaming loner. He loved art both in and outside school, and would spend the majority of his free time painting alone in his room.

However, as with Ian Brown, music was a large part of his early life. His parents were quite young and listened to the pop music of the time. So it was the sound of the Beatles,

Elvis, and Peggy Lee that filled the Squire household and these pop influences remained an integral part of John's musical psyche when he turned to composing.

"I didn't hear a bad song until I left home," remembered Squire. "I always consider the Beatles almost otherworldly. The fact that they grew up in a northern working-class environment and still made it, showed that you didn't have to come from London or America to make it."

The Beatles' hometown of Liverpool is just 30 miles from Manchester; however, Manchester considers itself the senior partner in the country's industrial north-west.

The friendship between Brown and Squire developed through a mutual interest in punk and the catalyst, ironically, were bands that came from London, such as The Clash and the Sex Pistols.

The Adverts were another early influence. They were formed in mid-1976 shortly after the first Sex Pistols gig by two art students from Devon—bassist, Gaye Atlas (a.k.a. Gaye Advert), and Tim "TV" Smith, on vocals (who had a successful post-punk career as a singer-songwriter, releasing the critically lauded *March of the Giants*). The other members included drummer, Laurie Driver, and guitarist, Howard Pickup. Seeing the Adverts at London's Roxy Club in Covent Garden, the Damned's guitarist, Brian James, invited them to open on the Damned's forthcoming UK tour. This led to them signing to the UK's new punk label, Stiff Records.

They played "Bored Teenagers" on a live compilation album recorded at the Roxy and released on the Harvest label. Their first single, "One-Chord Wonders," was released by Stiff on April 22, 1977. Moving to the bigger Anchor label, they released their next single, the ground-breaking "Gary Gilmore's Eyes" in July 1977. Double-murderer Gilmore had fought for the right to be executed, achieving his ambition in January 1977 at the hands of a Utah firing squad. He was the subject of Norman Mailer's 1979 novel *The Executioner's Song*. The Adverts' song told the imaginative tale of a man who receives Gilmore's eyes as a transplant and wakes from the operation looking through the eyes of a killer. It reached number 18 in the UK charts and was one of the first punk singles to achieve any measure of commercial success. But from then on, things went down hill. They released another single, "Safety in Numbers," and the album, *Crossing The Red Sea*, in February 1978. With its first 250 copies pressed in bright red vinyl, it is seen as a classic of British punk. After a number of changes of label and personnel, the band broke up in 1979, although Smith formed the Explorers soon after. *The Best of The Adverts* was released in 1998.

It was the anti-establishment lure of punk that drew John Squire and Ian Brown together, even though they lived in the same street and were now at the same high school.

"I didn't get to know him until punk," said Squire. "He was somebody local who was into the same music. We'd swap records and things … At the time, it felt like an illicit underworld."

Squire explained how punk inspired him: "I think London punk bands had more of an effect on my motivation, than [those from] where I was from. The whole ethos of The Clash, Pistols, all that era, and the fact that they promoted themselves on the platform of 'anyone can do it.' I don't know if that was true, but it certainly made me think that maybe I could. This wasn't personal advice, it was advice from the TV: Joe Strummer from The Clash turning to camera in a very stoic move was asked if he had any advice for the kids out there and he said, 'Believe in yourself, you can do anything you want.' That one went in and stayed."

Squire became obsessed with The Clash. Being a would-be artist, he was particularly fond of their painted trousers.

A few weeks after Brown had bought their debut album, *The Clash*, he went round to John Squire's house to find that Squire had painted a mural of Clash front man Joe Strummer covering an entire wall of the bedroom. Brown, however, was more into The Stranglers and The Jam, although this only served to broaden Squire's musical taste.

"It was definitely a case of opposites attract," said Squire. "He had records I didn't. He was more popular, yeah. I was happy to be a loner. I prefer it. We hung about for a short period, then when we started the band it became more permanent."

Squire had begun to play the guitar at 15 and was still in the early stages of learning to master it. But now listening to some of punk's great guitarists—Mick Jones from The Clash and Steve Jones from the Sex Pistols in particular—Squire was inspired to practice long and hard.

"'God Save The Queen' really made me want to start learning to play guitar," he said. "There's a low note, probably an A-string, just before the beginning of the second verse, really fat and thick. One note. Raw sex. I heard that and had to go and do it for myself. I was already into The Clash when I heard that."

Squire even went for a few professional guitar lessons. But it was a simple invention of his father's that really allowed his playing to progress. An electrical engineer, Squire's dad hooked up a variable transformer to the record player. By adjusting the voltage, the record could be slowed down, and John could study each note, chord, and riff in minute detail.

"My dad took the transformer off my train set," said Squire. "It had a knob on it that controlled the acceleration. He rigged it up so that it controled the speed on the record deck. I used to just tune the guitar down and pick things out. It was so good when I got into Jimmy Page, Jimi Hendrix, and Eric Clapton because I could slow everything down and pick out the guitar lines. It was very helpful."

Both Squire and Brown followed punk rock avidly throughout their years at Altrincham Grammar School, where they befriended another huge Clash fan, Simon "Si" Wolstencroft. He had already been drumming in other local bands around Manchester. He was reasonably experienced and had spent a lot of time in rehearsal rooms refining his craft by accompanying musicians a lot older than himself.

After Squire, Brown and Wolstencroft had passed their O-level examinations in 1979, they moved on together to South Trafford College, to study for A-Level examinations. By this time, Squire was becoming a competent guitarist and Brown had brought a bass guitar and could play a few riffs. At the beginning of 1980, the three of them decided to form a band. They would meet up at Si's house with their instruments. Si had his drum kit set up in his bedroom where they jammed together. Slowly they came up with some rough tunes, very much in the style of The Clash. They even came up with a suitable punk-style name.

"The Patrol was my first band, formed with John Squire and Ian Brown in the last year at Altrincham Grammar School," recalled Wolstencroft.

Squire, Brown, and Wolstencroft jammed together for most of their first year at college. By then they felt confident enough to perform in front of an audience, but they realized that before the band could play a live gig they would need a singer.

The band's first singer was another nominally non-Mancunian named Andy Couzens. He was born in 1962 in Stockport, which was six miles from Manchester, but still very much part of the conurbation.

"Stockport's like a village, it's weird," said Couzens. "My parents moved every two years, always within the Stockport area and then out to Macclesfield"—a small town ten miles to the south in rural Cheshire. "I was always moving school, which didn't make life easy. I couldn't wait to get out. I finished school and went as far away as I could, which was Altrincham."

He too turned up at South Trafford College in the Altrincham district of Manchester where he would come to the attention of Brown, Squire, and Wolstencroft. The three members of The Patrol were all still firmly rooted in the mindset of punk and wanted a front man who would embody the traits that punk singers should have—namely, rebelliousness, hooliganism, and more than a little craziness. They did not have to look far. He was already at their college.

As Couzens recalled: "I'd seen them lot in there but I never really spoke to them. We just walked past each other in the corridors giving each other the eye, me and Ian. You know, like, 'Who the fuck are you?'"

It was not until late in the year that the aspiring musicians approached Couzens. What brought them together was a piece of pure punk.

"I had a fight in the canteen," said Couzens. "Some fucking lad the night before had given my little brother a bit of a going over, so I laid him out. He was crying by the time I had finished. It was the first fight I'd had for ages. But it was at lunchtime with a load of people watching. There was a stunned silence."

Brown and Wolstencroft witnessed the altercation. At South Trafford College, everyone was grown up and well behaved. But here was Couzens, an outsider who broke all the rules. He admitted: "You just didn't do that at college—we were supposed to be in further education and beyond all that."

He was a rebel and a misfit, and handy with his fists—a very desirable quality in a front man in the early days of UK punk. Immediately after the fight, Brown and Wolstencroft approached him.

"Ian spoke first," Couzens recalled. "Simon Wolstencroft was there as well. He was into the later Clash look—creepers, crombies, quiff, neckerchiefs and all that 'London Calling' look."

The offer to join The Patrol as a singer came out of the blue. Couzens was "gob-smacked."

"I did this lad in and then I got myself a brew and some lunch and they asked me if I could sing," Couzens remembered. "I always wanted to be in a band and I wasn't aware they had a band. I was always going to see punk bands, but I couldn't play anything. They came over and said, 'Can you sing?' and I said, 'I'll have a go, yeah.'"

There was, perhaps, a more cynical reason Brown, Squire, and Wolstencroft wanted Couzens to join The Patrol. They had no transportation and he had a car—at least that was the way Si Wolstencroft remembered it.

"Andy Couzens was asked to sing to start with because his wealthy parents bought him an MG sports car when he went to South Trafford College, which we all attended for a while," said Wolstencroft. "It was a big novelty at the time."

Nevertheless, the canteen fight became incorporated into the band's legend, perhaps because it made a better story. But the car came in very useful for at least one other band member when Couzens attended his first rehearsal.

"I arranged to meet Ian just outside Timperley train station," said Couzens. "I was driving by then. They rehearsed in the back bedroom of Si's house in Hale Barns [south-west of the city]."

At that time, Couzens did not even know John Squire, as he said: "The first time I ever met John was at that rehearsal. I had seen him around at college. I thought there's that fucking Clash clone."

The influence of punk on the band was obvious.

"The music we were starting to do in The Patrol was loosely based on The Clash," admitted Wolstencroft. "Squire and myself were massive fans at the time. We left college to follow them round the country on the '16 Tons' tour in 1980."

However, Brown was already moving on. He had become a fan of The Jam, a band formed by Paul Weller, in 1973, which sparked a Mod revival in the late 1970s. Although The Jam shared their stripped-down, high-speed style with other punk bands, with Weller at the helm they were far superior as musicians, and in appearance they adopted the Mod-look of the mid-1960s. Although consistent hit-makers in the UK, they made little impression in the US until their 1981 album, *The Gift*, and the minor US hit, "Town Called Malice." They broke up in October 1982 and Paul Weller went on to form the Style Council the following year.

Despite a potential clash of musical styles, The Patrol was already coming together. Couzens was impressed: "They had a couple of bits of music, although they had had a few jams before I got there. Si had a good kit and he could play. John was pretty good, but it was all Clash-copy stuff. He played a bit of lead as well. He'd had proper guitar lessons. Ian was on bass and couldn't really play. He was a proper punk bass player. All fast strumming."

Andy Couzens may have thought Ian's bass playing was not up to scratch, but his own singing skills were non-existent. He plugged a microphone in the amp and simply shouted the lyrics over the backing—in true punk fashion.

"John had brought some lyrics with him that he thought I might want to sing," Couzens recalled. "It was a real Clash/reggae-type of thing called 'Gaol Of The Assassins.'"

Squire had also made a thumbnail character sketch of the members of The Patrol. As far as Couzens was concerned: "Ian was cocky, Si was always quiet. John was dead serious, with a lot of presence about him."

At that first gig, Couzens was quickly filled in on the band's history so far.

"John was the one who got it together initially," recalled Couzens. "They all went to Altrincham Grammar and had gone through discovering punk and all that sort of thing together, so it grew from there really."

There was a potential character clash between the pugilistic Andy Couzens and the aggressively self-possessed Ian Brown. For Couzens: "Ian was cocky as fuck right from the word go, trying to vibe me out. I wasn't having any of it. I remember saying to him, 'So you are a fucking Mod, are you? What's all that about?'"

It was respect for Squire that kept Couzens on side, as he said: "The thing I remember about John the most was that he was very typically artistically natured, quiet and shy. He always has a fringe to hide behind. I remember thinking he was quite interesting, you know."

Regardless of the clash of characters, the early Patrol rehearsals at Si's house went well. In a band environment, Squire's guitar playing improved and Wolstencroft's solid drumming developed into a solid base for their increasingly confident ensemble playing. All four of them worked hard on developing the songs and all of them really wanted to perform, so they upped their rehearsal schedule.

"We started rehearsing a few times every week," said Couzens. "That was one thing we always did. We rehearsed every night. We never really had a night off. We would do it all the time, live and breathe it. It's the only way to get things done. I remember the songs were all real Clash-type things. '25 Rifles,' 'Too Many Tons' named after The Clash's '16 Tons' tour. It was all real Clash stuff. I did a few lyrics, but they were mainly John's. It was all punk rock nonsense really."

As the band started to become proficient musicians and began building a catalogue of songs, a young friend named

Pete Garner sat in on their rehearsals. When they first started playing gigs he would be their roadie, then later he joined the band.

"Si was into Topper" (The Clash's second drummer, Nicky "Topper" Headon), said Garner. "He was aspiring to that sort of level really. Ian's bass playing was pretty rudimentary, classic punk style. And Squire's guitar was really Clash."

Pete Garner was a year younger than the other band members, but he lived in Timperley near Ian and John. He had met them years earlier at a place where local kids would kill time in the evenings. It was a bridge in the fields to the north of Sylvan Avenue, known simply as The Bridge. It was the home of the teenage alienation that is the basis of their music.

"The Bridge was like a meeting point," said Garner. "When everyone was ten or 11 they would hang out there and when they got to about 14, I guess they found something better to do and moved on."

Like Brown and Squire, Garner was estranged from the others by being sent to a different school.

"I was at Burnage High School and they were at South Trafford College," he said. "I didn't go to college and I had a lot of work to do to keep in the gang. You just don't speak to people in the year below and from a totally different school."

But then they met up again and started talking about music. Again it was punk that brought them together.

"We bonded over the punk thing," Garner recalled. "John was quiet, he didn't say much. He was really into The Clash while Ian was more into the Pistols and The Jam. We all thought that we were the king punks of the area. Ian and John would turn up and we'd give each other shit. I guess at some point there must have been some sort of mutual respect."

Garner's musical tastes were similar to Brown's and, as a big Clash fan, he found himself accepted by the other band members, even though they were older. But while it was Squire who was most obsessed with The Clash, it was Ian and Pete who got to meet them. They had heard that The Clash were going to record their new single in Manchester, and Brown and Gardner were naïve enough to think that if they hung around town they would get to see them. Squire did not accompany them, perhaps because he did not believe that hard-core Londoners such as The Clash would record in Manchester, or maybe he simply though that it would be impossible to find them in a city of half-a-million people. But Brown and Garner were made of sterner stuff. Undaunted, they set off for town.

"We got a train into town," said Garner. "We didn't know where they were going to be. Ian said there was a studio around there somewhere. It was pissing with rain. We thought this was ridiculous. Then this car pulled up and The Clash got out."

Brown remembered it slightly differently: "We were in town in Granby Row, where Pluto Studio was, we heard these drums and it turned out it was The Clash doing 'Bankrobber.' So we knocked on the door. They let us in, and we hung around for a day. They were nice. Topper was just regular. Strummer was a bit of a weirdo. He sat under this grandfather clock, clicking his fingers in time with it. I thought, what a dick."

Despite the other differences in their accounts, Garner recalled the finger-clicking too: "The one thing about

Strummer I remembered was that he was clicking his fingers to the clock. "I thought he was a bit fucking nuts till I went to a studio to record and realized about studio time."

Strummer's finger-clicking was supposed to remind the other band members that they were wasting expensive studio time. He was urging them on.

While the early Roses were great Clash fans, later The Clash returned the compliment.

"I saw Strummer being interviewed on TV just after I left the Roses," said Garner (who quit amicably shortly before the band made it big). "They asked him if he liked any bands and he said the Roses. I choked on my brew. I wanted to speak to John and say 'Jesus!' Strummer had picked up on the Roses just when the album came out and we were still really underground. I'd love to meet him and tell him me and Ian had met him one time."

But that was years later. For now the members of the Clash-inspired Patrol were trying to align their musical tastes to create a sound more of their own.

"We were all into the same stuff," recalled Couzens. "Generation X's first album was a big one with all of us. We listened to everything from glam, to skin, to punk. We all delved into Johnny Thunders and the New York Dolls separately from each other. It was a real meeting of the minds. We all had a core of stuff we really liked. We branched off into our own stuff as well. I was into Joy Division and the others weren't."

Joy Division was a punk band formed in Manchester in 1977, who took their name from World War II Nazi prostitutes. They had hits in the UK with "She's Lost Control," "Transmission," and "Temptation." These appear on the *Unknown Pleasures* album, produced by Martin Hannett, who went on to produce The Stone Roses' early singles and an unreleased album, before their debut with *The Stone Roses*. Joy Division were the backbone of Factory, Manchester's up-and-coming record label, and a cornerstone of the Manchester music scene. Following the suicide of their lead singer Ian Curtis, they became New Order. In 1983, they released "Blue Monday," the biggest-selling 12-inch single of all time in the UK. This was remixed by Quincy Jones, giving them a top-five hit. They also scored a number one in the UK with the soccer anthem "World in Motion" in 1990.

"I remember turning John on to some of the early Joy Division stuff," said Couzens. "I had two copies of the first EP. I gave John one. He was bang into it."

Garner recalled that much of their rehearsal time was taken up by discussing other music: "That was so important. We knew so much about music. We talked about it all the time. We knew everything. It was an obsession."

Despite their musical discussions, they got on with the business of rehearsing and were soon ready to go on stage. The Patrol played their first gig on Friday, March 28, 1980. The venue was a local youth club, Sale Annex Youth Club, and tickets only cost 30p (50 cents). Sale is another urban center in south-west Manchester a few miles from Timperley. It was the club's punk rock night and other local bedroom bands, Suburban Chaos and Corrosive Youth, were also on the bill. But although it was their first gig, The Patrol were the headliners and watched the others before they went on.

"Our first gig was at Sale Annex in some youth club in the middle of Sale, a really grotty youth club," said Couzens. "A couple of other bands played. A punk band from Stretford played as well. I can't remember their name, a proper noisy punk band."

When they finally got on stage The Patrol were well received. As Couzens recalled: "We went down pretty good—we were shocked. We had been rehearsing so much it was as good as that stuff was going to get. Ian was doing his thing, sucking in the youth culture, that's what he's really good at. We were all looking more Clash-like. Me and Ian had short hair. I was jumping around. John used to move as well in a Mick Jones style."

Of the line-up that night, the members of The Patrol were particularly impressed by Suburban Chaos, who dressed as hardcore punks, sporting studded leather jackets and spikey Mohican hairstyles. They played a far brasher, far louder brand of punk rock than they did. The Patrol, by comparison, were more melodic and a bit more together as a band.

As Suburban Chaos were thrashing their way through violent songs, Garner realized that he recognized them: "When we arrived at the gig, I thought 'hang on, I know these guys.' It turned out that a year before I was at some disco dancing to some punk records and these punks had piled in and kicked me in the face. I got up trying to sort them out and they just looked at me. There were loads of them so I left it at that. And it turns out that they had become Suburban Chaos."

However at the gig in Sale Annex Youth Club, the two bands got on. Afterwards they realized that they quite liked each other and decided to arrange some more local gigs together.

"Suburban Chaos had a song called 'Anarchy In The Suburbs', which was their anthem," said Couzens. "They were all right. I mean everyone was 16 at the time. We all became mates. They were Stretford lads; we were Sale lads. It was a bit like West Side Story!" Stretford is inside the city limits of Manchester, just north of Sale.

The Patrol played their second gig on May 15, 1980 in Lymm, a small village out to the west of South Manchester around halfway to Warrington. Suburban Chaos supported them and soon became their regular support. It was a crucial turning point. Briefly, toward the end of the gig, The Stone Roses future line-up appeared for the first time together on stage, with Pete Garner taking over on bass, while Ian Brown sang one number, and Andy Couzens moved out of the limelight onto rhythm guitar. And already they found they were beginning to build a following.

"We played a village hall out in Lymm and a youth club in Stretford to a bunch of glueheads and punks—probably 15 to 30 people there but it felt full. They ended up following us around," said Couzens. "We had about eight songs by then."

Hale Methodist Church was another local venue.

Squire remembered: "We did a Cockney Rejects' cover called 'I'm Not A Fool.'"

After that, The Patrol played a gig to a home crowd at South Trafford College where they still studied between rehearsals. This time they appeared without the support of Suburban Chaos, but there were a few other college bands on the bill.

"The day after the Lymm gig we played at South Trafford College," said Couzens. "There were a couple of college metal bands supporting—Firecloud and something else."

The performance went well and wowing their classmates gave the band the self-confidence to record a demo.

"We did a demo that was limited to 100 copies," recalled Brown, "but I don't have it anymore. All my stuff got nicked years later so I don't have a copy myself. We did a song called 'Gaol Of The Assassins' and another called '25 Rifles.'"

Couzens also recalled the demo they did as The Patrol: "There were three songs, 'Too Many Tons,' 'Gaol Of The Assassins,' and '25 Rifles.' They were recorded in Rusholme studio just off Great Western Street where Mick Hucknall did a lot of stuff with his punk band the Frantic Elevators," he said. "The only reason I know this was because we met him in there."

In 1984, Mick Hucknall quit the Frantic Elevators and found fame with Simply Red. They broke through in the US with the chart-topping "Holding Back The Years" in 1986.

After The Patrol had laid down their demo, they did a few more local shows. On July 11, 1980 the band played a gig in Lostock—a small town ten miles south of Manchester's suburbs in Cheshire. There they were supported again by Suburban Chaos and Corrosive Youth. By this time The Patrol were beginning to learn their stagecraft, which they honed as they played more gigs throughout the summer of 1980. Soon Brown began to develop his distinctive confrontational style.

"Ian always had to have a microphone so he could shout at people," said Couzens. "It was funny. It was good for a laugh. We played at the college and played the Portland Bars in town as well."

Their debut in the city center Portland Bars was a breakthrough.

As Couzens recalled: "It was our first proper gig with a PA and it was a total shock, total. I could hear myself."

They began supporting established bands at well-known venues. And The Patrol itself began to get a bit of local recognition. Legend has it that they once nearly replaced Adam And The Ants, then a major punk band of the late 1970s in the UK, latterly managed by the ubiquitous Malcolm McLaren, who never really caught on in the US.

"That was the gig I booked for them," said Garner. "When The Ants should have played the Osbourne. I rang up to see what time The Ants were playing, but they hadn't made it. I said I know a band that could play; I'll get them down. Ian and Andy said brilliant but we couldn't find John anywhere. It turns out that he was sat in a field being artistic. It would have been a bad idea anyway. They were too young, a bunch of 16-year-olds playing to an early Ants crowd—big Mohican crazies. Can't see it working!"

Anyway, the Patrol had come close to playing in front of their first truly large crowd. Years later Garner continued to speculate on how the history of The Stone Roses would have been altered if they had played that gig: "Maybe The Patrol would have continued and The Stone Roses never have come into existence."

Instead on August 8, The Patrol played a gig in Dunham Massey—a town a few miles west of Altrincham—with their regular support of Suburban Chaos and Corrosive Youth. Then, on November 14, they played what would be their last gig as The Patrol at their college.

Although they continued to rehearse together after that last South Trafford College gig, there was a growing dissatisfaction within the band and a general feeling that they wanted to strike out in a new direction.

"We decided we were going to change it all," said Couzens. "We were still rehearsing after the last gig. We were all trying to push it forward. We weren't going to push it any further forward with what it was …"

Playing together on stage, in front of an audience, had changed their approach.

Couzens continued: "We had done a few gigs and towards the end the music had started to change slightly. It went away from The Clash thing, more rock 'n' roll for want of a better phrase. We were getting into Johnny Thunders, really drifting that way—John was pushing it that way."

But it was not just Squire's influence that led to these new musical developments. As a band, The Patrol began to work together as a unit.

"It's funny how bands work, you feed off each other," recalled Couzens. "Playing off each other's stuff, arguing, and something gets spat out. You might have a riff, but the other person can't play it, or someone starts singing along with it."

Under the pressure of these musical developments, The Patrol began to fall apart. As Couzens remembered: "First of all we got another guitar player in, I can't remember his name, but I had to sack him because John and Ian wouldn't dare. This guy was on rhythm guitar. I think this was before Ian got to be singer. I've a feeling he was called Neil, I'm not sure. He was a bit of a beer monster. One of those types. I said to John, I can play the guitar instead. I can't sing! I never could. I never professed to, so I moved to guitar."

It was true that Couzens' singing talents were laughable. Brown, then the bassist, wanted to take over the vocals and the band decided that he could at least carry a tune. Couzens jumped at the opportunity to play rhythm guitar, which he felt suited him better. Meanwhile their roadie Pete Garner was itching to join the band on stage. Garner had followed the band diligently and had already played bass for them once before—at the end of the Lymm gig earlier that summer. Ian Brown had closed that gig with his first singing performance, a rendition of The Sweet's "Blockbuster." And he had passed his bass guitar to Garner who strummed his way through the simple riff.

"I had never played bass before," said Garner. "They showed me the riff to 'Blockbuster' and I just got up and hammed my way through it. It was the last time I played bass for years."

For the duration of that song The Stone Roses as would be were on stage. Back in the rehearsal room they would experiment with that new line up again.

"So Ian went on vocals," said Couzens. "I learned a few chords from John, and Pete came in on bass, just for a few rehearsals and then that fell to pieces again … By now we had a bit of a PA, when we turned it up, it fed back. Everyone was shouting at the guitar players 'too loud!'"

Ian Brown was now the band's front man. It was the place he was suited by temperament to be. It was a place he could be adored.

don't stop

Even though with their new line-up that put Ian Brown on vocals and Pete Garner on bass The Patrol seemed to have a new direction, the band began to rehearse less often. Squire became apathetic had hung around at home in his bedroom slippers.

As Couzens recalled: "We used to call round for John and he'd be in his pathetic slipper phase and his brother Matt would come out instead. Matt is just like John but a laugh. John would be in his bedroom making models when you'd go round. He was one of those guys who would melt plastic cars so they would look like they'd had a crash. You think, how's he done that? They were all painted up afterwards, fucking brilliant."

Occasionally they could persuade Squire to come out.

"We were still mates," said Couzens, "because we continued to go out with each other and hang out—one, two or three of us—one night rehearsing, the next night not."

By now, most of the band members had finished college and had to find work.

"I do remember Ian got a job working at the DHSS [the Department of Health and Social Services distributes dole money to the unemployed] in Sale," said Couzens. "Pete was working anyway in Paperchase [a chain of stationers] in town. John was for a long time sat at home making models. Si had a job in a fish shop in Wilmslow, and he started doing stuff with Andy Rourke and Johnny Marr. He did those demos with them."

Rourke and Marr were founder members of The Smiths, another key Manchester band. Formed in 1982, The Smiths achieved cult status in the US with their third album *The Queen Is Dead* in 1986.

Soon Brown lost interest in the band completely. The others drifted into other things and The Patrol disbanded. Ian sold his bass guitar and brought himself a motor scooter. Music, for him, had been an adolescent distraction. Or so he thought.

"It wasn't serious," said Brown. "I never really wanted to be in a group so I sold my bass and got a scooter with the money—£100 [$150]."

The Italian motor scooter—particularly the Lambretta and Vespa—was a key icon in the Mod culture of the early 1960s that was being revived at the time. Brown found himself embracing Mod culture and mixing it in with his punk influences. The Mod lifestyle seemed to offer broader horizons. His scooter gave him independence and freedom, and he spent the next few years in local scooter clubs— largely a gang of like-minded youths—riding across the country, visiting seaside towns and getting into fights. Ever with itchy feet, Ian would later travel farther afield, backpacking through Europe.

Although Brown was a fan of The Jam and rode around the UK on a scooter, he denied being a Mod: "The scooter boys were not Mods, we were a mixture of punks, skins, anyone who had a scooter. I used to see Clinton from Pop Will Eat Itself [a punk band from Stourbridge outside Birmingham] on scooter runs. We used to get attacked by bikers in Stourbridge till we followed Clinton down an alternative safe route. The police would pull me up wherever I went. I was once fined £20 [$30] for having condensation on my speedometer."

Eventually Couzens and Squire got into scooters as well.

"I had a Lambretta," said Couzens, who admitted that he did this under the influence of Brown. "Ian had the first scooter. I went with Ian to buy a Lambretta."

But Brown had problems with his own machine.

Couzens continued: "He's one of those people who breaks everything. Ian can't wear a watch, or anything mechanical. He breaks anything when he goes near it. He bought this Lambretta and it never worked for him at all. It never went. He was completely incapable with it. The thing is with Lambrettas is that they don't fucking work. It's like owning an old motorbike. You have to take it apart and clean it. I could do that but he couldn't do it all, so he went out and bought a Vespa."

In fact Brown had two Lambrettas before getting his Vespa. His first scooter had been a Lambretta J125, but he soon exchanged it for a different one.

"Yeah, that was a Lambretta GP200," said Brown. "It had extended forks, banana seat, leg shields off." And it was painted pink! "Sweet And Innocent, it was called. And I had a Vespa Rally 200 with 'Angels With Dirty Faces' painted on the side. I had five or six over time. We went to all the rallies—Brighton, the Isle of Wight, Scotland, Great Yarmouth."

The Vespa was a more reliable machine and he risked traveling farther afield on it. In fact, during his time as a scooter boy, Brown claimed that he visited every seaside town in Great Britain.

While proto-Mods Brown and Couzens were turning to scooter-culture, Squire was being an artist full time. But eventually he followed suit.

"Two years later, I got John into it," said Brown. "He had a GP200 that he made up himself."

The scooter also benefitted from Squire's artistic attentions.

As Couzens pointed out: "John bought a Lambretta, he didn't ride it that much, but spent a lot of time pulling it apart, painting it, getting everything copper-plated. You can say each bike was a reflection of the owner's personality."

Across the petrol tank, Squire's scooter had emblazoned The Clash lyric: "Too Chicken To Even Try It." Squire claimed that it was as a medium for artistic expression that got him into the scooter scene.

"A Lambretta is a very desirable object," said Squire. "Ian wanted one. I got one. Did it up, painted it. I wanted to show it off to other people who had scooters."

Like Brown, Squire enjoyed getting on his scooter and riding into a seaside resort with a bunch of other Mods and other scooter boys.

"It felt like we taking over the town," said Squire.

Mod culture was taking over completely from punk at the time, especially with the release of the classic cult movie *Quadrophenia* (1979), starring Gordon Matthew Sumner (a.k.a. Sting). The movie depicted conflicts between Mods and Rockers—British bikers—in the south coast resort of Brighton in 1964. Accompanied by The Who's album *Quadrophenia*, it revived interest in the whole scene and made Mod the height of fashion again. But not everyone was so willing to change.

"I was still the punk in the crowd," recalled Pete Garner, "and I was still hanging out with them. But we would go to

Mod parties and people wouldn't let me in because of my punk clothes. It got to be a real drag."

Consequently, Mod revival polarized the group. Brown and Squire were into the Fred-Perry-casual look and bombing around with a Stockport scooter club or Chorlton Gladiators, a scooter gang who wore distinctive rabbit's tails that ran from the front to the back of their crash helmets—a forerunner of the strange headgear Brown would later wear on stage. The move to Mod culture also broadened the band members' musical taste, as in the early 1960s, Mods were into the Motown sound.

"I used to go to Northern Soul all-nighters in Rhyl, Rotherham, and Doncaster," Brown remembered. "Very into it I was. All through the night till late in the morning. It was either that, New Romantics, or long raincoats."

The flamboyantly theatrical style of the New Romantics—whose foremost exponent Boy George was the only real artist to conquer the US—found little following in the north of England, where a grittier style was favoured.

Squire's taste was broadening too. He hung out in Manchester's Pips club, where they had different rooms that played Northern Soul, Roxy Music, David Bowie, or oldies. Meanwhile Garner and the others were left wallowing in the ennui of punk. But music remained a common link between them all. Even though their tastes were changing, there was a lot of new music that they all liked, especially what was happening on the vibrant Manchester scene.

While Brown got deeper into the world of scooter gangs, Squire turned away and got back into music with a vengeance. He would stay indoors and kept practicing guitar.

Now he really started to develop as a guitarist, not just imitating The Clash riffs anymore, but building up his own unique style—adding a new, broadly Mod sensibility. His time with the scooter clubs had opened his ears to the sounds of the 1960s. Asked what his state of mind was at that the time, Squire described it as "progressive—never satisfied with where I am or what I'd done."

Wolstencroft was still into music too. He was playing in a band called Freaky Party with Andy Rourke and Johnny Marr. It was from that springboard, they would go on to form The Smiths. Meanwhile, direction-less, Brown took a job in a local hotel.

"The first thing I did was scrub pots," he said. "Been left school two days and I'm in this big oven in a hotel with the chef kicking me. That's when I realized I didn't want a job. I stood it about three weeks."

After that he went traveling the UK on his scooter, although sometime he ventured farther afield, hitch-hiking his way around Europe.

"I've always been on the move," explained Brown. "When I lived in Sale I never hung about there. I hung about with lads all over the city. I've been to every seaside resort in England and most cities. I've been to most of Europe, just moving about. It's what I'm into doing."

For Brown, his relentless urge to be on the move was part of a rite of passage he would later describe in the track "Made Of Stone." He traveled, but he still had no clear direction. And though he had no clear idea of what he wanted to do with his life, he knew what he did not want to do.

"I never wanted to work on a building site or go to university," he recalled. "I didn't think what I was going to do. I just drifted. I'm still drifting."

Garner still worked for Paperchase in the center of Manchester, while Couzens was still at college—until his academic career was cut short by an unfortunate incident.

"I got thrown out of college," said Couzens. "I took a swing at a teacher and told the principal to go and fuck himself. The rest of the band had finished college and they all had passed."

Having failed to graduate, Couzens dropped off the band's radar screen for a while.

As well as practicing his music, Squire got a job in Cosgrove Hall—an animation workshop that produced cult British TV shows such as *Wind In The Willows* and *Dangermouse*—although he made no big claims about his contribution.

"I wasn't working as an illustrator," he said. "I was in the Mud Pie Department."

He made models for *Wind In The Willows*. However, it seems that Squire's artistic talents were put to even better use designing Bertie Bassett, the legendary mascot of Bassett's Liquorice Allsorts. The sweet company use the animated figure of Bertie Bassett, who is made out of a collection of their variously shaped and highly colored confections, in their TV commercials to this day.

With Brown off exploring the UK on his scooter and Squire busy at work, there was little contact between the band members. However, Squire still needed paints and paper and Garner occasionally served him in Paperchase, while Couzens also kept in loose contact with Squire.

"We didn't see each other for what seemed like ages but it was probably six weeks," said Couzens. "I remember going out with John one night. We went to a pub in Sale, which was weird because no one drank. We decided then to get something else going on."

Couzens wanted to start a new band and convinced Squire to join him: "It must have been later in the year, I went around and said, 'let's do something,' because I love it, the band thing. The Patrol was gone and I wanted to do something so John and I started another band up with a guy from Hale, a drummer—a good drummer who popped up in a few bands later on. His name was Guy I think; good looking guy. Me and John were playing guitar, and Ian was off on his scooters."

At this point in time, Brown was not even aware that Couzens and Squire had formed a band again and he played no part in it.

"The core was me and John rehearsing in Warrington," said Couzens. "I haven't a clue why we went there. It's really vague this period. We rehearsed above the YMCA opposite the town hall gates. There was that lad from Hale on the drums sometimes. There was also another guy later on called Walt from Lymm in there as well. He was useless—a proper punk drummer—and we were trying to do something a bit more together musically. We got into the Beach Boys, although there was a lot of stuff like Generation X still getting listened to. I lent John my Beach Boys' *Greatest Hits;* you know the one with the blue cover with the surfer on it. We liked the songs— they were a bit more musical than punk. We were trying to get the music going, nothing else. No one singing."

Incorporated into this loose outfit of musicians was Gary "Mani" Mountfield, who explained: "I met John at the Northern Soul room at Pips and I met Ian in the fight against Fascism—through my little gang of scooter boys in north Manchester. We were having trouble with this gang of local skinheads. The word went out to Ian's south Manchester crew, who came over. We joined forces and hospitalized them."

Bassist, Mani, was to become the final addition to the classic Stone Roses' line up. He was born on November 16, 1962 in Moston, north Manchester.

"I'm a north Manchester boy," said Mani, "originally from Moston but I moved to Failsworth and Newton Heath in my early teens and I still go there for a beer because that's where all my mates are."

North Manchester was a world away from the south of the city where the rest of the band's members lived. The north was a blue collar area; the lads were tough and working class. The south was leafy and suburban; kids there went to college.

As well as knowing Squire, and now Couzens, Mani crucially had connections with Ian Brown. They had met up during a fight when gangs from both the north and south of the city joined up to sort out a local bully who had been terrorizing kids in the northern Manchester estates.

"I'd known Mani from when he was 16," Brown said. "He was from north Manchester; we were from Chorlton. We'd heard about this kid with a swastika on his head, some bonehead who lived near Mani's, who was bullying kids. So we got a crew up to sort him out. Twenty of us went to meet Mani's crew in this council house. I remember seeing Mani sat down. I'm thinking he ain't no fighter. So, one or two of these kids dealt with the bonehead, put him to rest, and that's how we met."

Mani recalled the occasion: "There were some National Front skinheads in north Manchester who'd been shakin' a lot of me mates up, so Ian Brown and a crew of his mates from south Manchester met up with us through a mutual friend and we went and dealt with them. We've been mates ever since."

The National Front are a neo-Fascist political party that sprung up in the 1970s and which specialized in exploiting the racial tensions caused by the economic downturn in the UK at that time.

This incident says everything about Brown—he was tough, principled, committed, and burning with idealism. Those qualities come through in tracks such as "Sugar Spun Sister," "How Do You Sleep," "Resurrection," and "Waterfall." These songs talk of injustice, betrayal, revenge, and insurrection. However, Brown made quite a different impression on Mani at that first encounter.

"I remember vividly meeting Ian and thinking, that kid looks like Galen off *Planet Of The Apes*," said Mani. "He always had that striking simian thing. And I liked him from day one because he looked like a character off my favorite telly program. Even now, his number in my book is under 'King Monkey.'"

Despite the circumstances of his first meeting with Ian Brown, Mani was definitely not a fighter. But like every other kid in Manchester he was obsessed with soccer.

As he said: "I'm proud to be a Manc, proud to be a Red [a fan of Manchester United, famous for their red shirts]. My dad was a mad United fan. Nobby Stiles is part of my family—my auntie's cousin or something like that ..."

Nobby Stiles was a famous Manchester United midfielder who played for England's national team in their celebrated victory over Germany in the final of the 1966 soccer World Cup.

"... I was born to be a Red. I would have had my ears boxed in if I'd dared to be a Blue," he continued.

The Blues are the rival Manchester City soccer club, so called because of their blue shirts.

"When I was a kid, I used to get the number seven bus from Failsworth which used to drop you off by the swing bridge," Mani recalled. This was the entrance to Manchester United's Old Trafford soccer ground. "It cost 50p to go in the Stretford End and I used to take our Greg, sit him on the barrier, give him his Wagon Wheels and crisps and then watched the match. When we were old enough, we used to get the specials [discounted season tickets] through the 1970s and 1980s. I didn't miss many matches. I used to go to away games all the time with a lot of those heads from Salford. I can remember going to Luton when we were on the ten-games winning streak in 1985. We met up at Salford Crescent, got in a car and went down to terrorize St Albans for the day. It's only in the past few years that I've cut down on going home and away."

Mani was one of the famed beer-swilling English soccer hooligans that were making headlines around the world at the time. But when he was young, like so many boys who live in big soccer towns, Mani wanted to find fame as a professional soccer player.

"My childhood hero was George Best," he said.

George Best, the legendary Manchester United and Northern Ireland player, was said by Brazilian soccer star,

Pelé, to be the greatest player ever. Unfortunately, he went on to become a legendary drinker.

"My mam and dad were mates of him," Mani said. "I can remember waking up in the morning and him being downstairs in my house having a late drink when he shouldn't have been."

Ian Brown was another fanatical Manchester United supporter and a fan of George Best. This common interest drew Mani and Brown together. Through Brown, Mani got to know Squire, Couzens, and the other members of The Patrol. At the same time they met up with Steve Cressa, who later became The Roses' dancer and effects man.

But however much Mani dreamed of being a soccer star, he knew he just was not up to following in the footsteps of his hero, George Best. Instead, music would be his calling.

Mani accepted this fact: "I was never good enough to be a footballer and I'm lucky that I make a living out of music."

But after graduating from Xaverian College, a Catholic high school, he was reluctant to go out and find regular employment.

"As for school, I went to Xaverian and after there I tried my hardest not to get a job and sat in my bedroom learning to play a guitar," he said. "I knew from the age of eight that I wanted to be in a band."

With dedicated practice, Mani quickly became a solid bass player. He was an asset to the new band Squire and Couzens were getting together and, later, to The Stone Roses. For band practice, Andy Couzens would pick him up in his MG and take him to the rehearsal rooms in Warrington. Mani would also accompany the boys on their nights out in the music venues around the city center.

However, as Couzens pointed out: "The band was going through a funny period, it didn't even have a name."

This amorphous rehearsal group soon fell apart, not least because of the long drive to Warrington. A year later Squire and Couzens would try to form yet another band. They were now familiar with Mani's excellent bass playing and brought him into the fold. In 1982, the three of them began rehearsing once more, this time in the basement of Couzens' parents' house in Macclesfield. The new band needed a singer, so they brought in a friend of Mani's from north Manchester, who the others vaguely knew from scooter clubs and nights out drinking. His name was David Kartley, but people called him Kaiser.

"We sort of knew Kaiser because we had been going out in town," Couzens explained. "He was part of our little drinking clique and a scooter boy as well."

Kaiser recalled how he came to be in the band: "I was hanging around in punk clubs like Berlin and the punk room in Pips, and there was me and Mani and some other lads from the scooter runs. It was John Squire that came over and started chatting. He said that he was starting a band up and asked me if I wanted to be the singer. At the time we all still liked the old punk stuff. Ian Brown, who was around but not in the band, was into Madness—he loved them."

Madness were a vaudevillian pop band from north London, formed in 1976. Their self-proclaimed "nutty sound" was applied to soul, R&B, and music-hall music, as well as ska, the pre-reggae Jamaican dance rhythm popular in the UK in the 1960s. Their name comes from a Prince Buster song. With songs such as "Baggy Trousers," "It Must Be Love,"

"Cardiac Arrest," "House of Fun," and "Our House," they became a top singles band in the UK from 1978 to 1983. Little was released in the US, but they developed a cult following in America for their zany concert performances. Their inventive lyrics and their conscious use of a regional—cockney—accent would be influential.

According to Kaiser: "John Squire was much more arty. None of us had ever heard of the stuff he was into, very strange! He was a very special type of person John, very artistic and he really put his mind to what he doing whether it was playing guitar or painting. He was working at Cosgrove Hall at the time. He took us down there a couple of times. He was making models there and he'd made a couple of adverts. He was very articulate. The people in the band were very varied from each other. John had a really different outlook on things compared to the rest of us."

Together Squire, Couzens, Mani, and Kaiser formed the nucleus of a new band. However, they still did not have a drummer, so all they could do was rehearse. They wanted to recruit their ex-Patrol drummer Wolstencroft, but he was now playing full time with Andy Rourke and Johnny Marr who were trying to start The Smiths. They were going to have to look elsewhere. Again it was Mani's north Manchester connections that came to the rescue. Mani brought in Chris Goodwin, a friend of his from Failsworth, to fill the drumming vacancy.

"I guess that the band was a continuation from the Warrington thing," said Couzens. "That band might have stopped for a few weeks and then the new one started. We didn't see much of Ian at the time. He was always on his scooter runs."

So now with a line-up set, they went about rehearsing hard in Couzens' basement. As he explained: "We used to rehearse in my parents' house in Macclesfield. I used to go and pick up John in Chorlton and then go up to pick up Mani and the rest of them. Musicians are fucking lazy, aren't they? I was always picking people up. I was the organizer. Drive around, pick everyone up, then rehearse."

Kaiser recalled how fun all this was at the time: "Andy came up to my house to pick me up in his BMW. You never got posh cars like that round our way. We practiced in Andy's house in a cellar. It was a big house in Adlington. A big mansion. An unbelievable place with a swimming pool. It was a real big shock to me and Mani. We had a great time just going in the swimming pool and hanging out with Andy and his brother who's a good lad."

It was this mixture of influences from the gritty, industrialized, working-class north of Manchester and the leafy suburban south that gave the new line-up their musical edge. That quality would be retained as the group developed into The Stone Roses and into *The Stone Roses* album itself.

As the new band started to come together musically, they called themselves, with little sense of irony, The Fireside Chaps. This seems to have been Squire's choice and did not really seem fitting.

Couzens felt that: "It wasn't something that we could ever contemplate putting on a poster. John Squire can be cringe-worthy when it comes to names."

At one time they called themselves, excruciatingly, English Rose—appropriately without Kaiser. Couzens explained: "I remember we changed our name to English

Rose, because of that Jam track we liked. Bloody diabolical we were. I was on vocals, John was a pretty basic guitar player back then. We were all kicking against it, really, trying to be Manchester's answer to the New York Dolls."

But they had competition closer to home. As Couzens pointed out: "People were all going mental about The Smiths, 'Oh, this is the best thing since sliced bread,' they'd say. And we fuckin' hated it. For us it had to be heavy."

Like The Fireside Chaps, English Rose never played a gig.

Unfortunately, just as The Fireside Chaps' first songs were coming together drummer Chris Goodwin left the band, but as things were going ahead so smoothly the rest of the band just carried on regardless, writing and rehearsing while the drum kit gathered cobwebs in the corner. In fact, the departure of their drummer did not affect the band adversely at all. It only succeeded in strengthening the resolve of the remaining members. Not only was their music developing well, but also they were becoming closer as friends.

Couzens recalled how they would rehearse together all week and then go out together on the weekends: "The rest of us were going out into town a lot. I seem to remember going to the Cypress Tavern, places like that. We went down to the Hacienda as soon as it opened. You know what's it like, fuck there is somewhere to go! When you're the only club in Manchester it's easy to get members. It was the only place to go. When it opened we ran down there to join really early on in 1982."

The Hacienda was opened in May 1982 by Howard Jones, after The Electric Circus, Manchester's premier punk venue, was forced to close. Jones had previously run a dive called Rafters that had hosted Elvis Costello, XTC, Slaughter And The Dogs, Rich Kids, and Magazine during the period that punk was transmuting into new wave. The new club was the idea of New Order's manager, Rob Gretton. Funded by Factory Records and New Order, the Hacienda quickly became the most famous club in the UK. A huge cavernous warehouse space in a semi-derelict part of town, it pioneered a new vogue for stripped down post-industrial interiors. Video jocks spliced together old black-and-white movies, bondage videos, and psychedelic effects. It played host to a number of the most notable bands of the era. However, it lost money almost every day it was open and finally closed in June 1997. The building was demolished 18 months later and bricks were sold for £5 ($7.50) each. The life of the Hacienda is now celebrated in the movie 24-Hour Party People.

Squire, Kaiser, Mani, and Couzens rehearsed all year and by the end of 1982 they decided to record a demo. It was then that they realized the name The Fireside Chaps would have to go. So the band had a brain-storming session to come up with a new name.

"One night, after rehearsing we sat down and watched Marlon Brando in the movie On The Waterfront," said Couzens. "We all thought Fireside Chaps was a funny name but when it came to the point of doing demos we thought fuck, can't put that on a demo tape on the tape box. So thanks to Marlon we took 'The Waterfront' for our name and went in and did the demo tracks. The demo was recorded somewhere in the back end of Denton—somewhere around Mani's way in a little studio someone had set up."

The demo was much more melodic than music from The Patrol's punk period. Squire's guitar playing had improved out of all recognition and Mani's bass playing kept the whole thing going in lieu of a drummer. Ian Brown recalled first hearing his friends' demo: "The Patrol was a racket so I'd got into scooters, but John was still doing his band. He played me a tape and it sounded really good. I was impressed that I knew somebody who could play with quality. Since '78 or '79 John hadn't done much except play guitar."

And it was not just Squire who impressed Brown. The whole band drew his praise.

"The Waterfront were great," he said. "They had a song called 'On The Beach In Normandy.'" The idea for the song came from Kaiser, but it was written in collaboration with Squire.

"John wrote most of the songs and I wrote some of the lyrics," said Kaiser. "'On The Beach In Normandy' was about a trip me and Mani made. We blagged our way to France jumping on trains, and we ended up in Normandy and we ended up walking down the beaches in Normandy. We were just Motson lads and we were gob-smacked, walking down there. I wrote the song about that and how thousands had died on those same beaches on D Day."

In "On The Beach In Normandy," they had taken the political awareness of British punk and moved it into mainstream pop. This would come to characterize much of the work of The Stone Roses and would be especially evident in many of the tracks on the album *The Stone Roses*.

By this time Ian Brown had left his parents' home and had moved into an apartment in Charles Barry Crescent, a dilapidated project in Hulme just south of Manchester city center and a world away from the leafy suburb of Timperley.

He was still in touch with the members of The Waterfront and hung out with them at the Hacienda and other clubs in the center of the city.

Then fate took a hand. Brown had a girlfriend named Mitch and on her 21st birthday in 1983, he held a party for her at his apartment. It was an open-door affair with music and people spilling out into the hallway. And into the flat that night walked the American soul-legend Geno Washington.

"I'm at my party in Hulme, my mate's roadying at Salford University," explained Brown, "and he brings Geno Washington down to this party."

Having come to the UK in the 1960s with the US Air Force, Washington and his Ram Jam Band and signed with Pye and had two of the biggest selling albums in the UK in that decade. In 1966, his *Funky Butt Live* stayed in the UK album charts for 48 weeks and was only outsold by Simon and Garfunkel's *Bridge Over Troubled Water*, and the soundtrack from *The Sound Of Music*. Staying on in the UK, Geno became a leading light on the Northern Soul scene in the 1980s, and Dexy's Midnight Runners' tribute to him, "Geno," had been to number one in the charts in 1980. Brown was thrilled to have a musician of Washington's standing at this party—and, apparently, Washington was impressed with Brown too.

"He's a superstar kind of guy—a big personality, all over the room," Brown said. "He comes up to me and he says, 'You're a star. You're an actor. Be a singer.'"

In fact, it was not the first time Brown had seen Geno Washington, who was a well-known character in the area: "I remember him on the street smoking a big spliff, and this copper comes around saying, 'What are you doing?' And he's blowing his spliff in the copper's face, this is in '83. And he's going, 'I'm Geno, man. Geno Geno!' singing the Dexy's song, really cool. And the copper didn't do nothing, he just walked away."

This irreverent attitude to authority was chimed in by Brown. Now, at the party, the man had actually spoken to him and what he said had to be taken seriously.

"A few weeks later, I'm thinking about what this guy's said," Brown recalled. "What does he mean I'm a star, an actor? A few days after that John rang up and asked me if I could sing and I thought, I'll go with that. I've got to. I just have to. Anyway, I thought we'd give it a go. We kicked Kaiser out and started the real thing, The Stone Roses, in March 1984."

this is the one

At the end of 1983, Ian Brown had joined The Waterfront. Kaiser had not been kicked out quite yet, and he and Ian would share vocals down in Couzens' basement. But eventually The Waterfront disintegrated. Their sound already seemed dated as The Smiths, New Order, and The Chameleons were taking the Manchester sound in a new direction.

"There was a gap between the bands [The Waterfront and The Stone Roses] because John was busy at Cosgrove Hall," noted Couzens. "He was always going home and making models. I remember taking John down to Cosgrove Hall in the car with a bunch of models."

At the time Squire was trying to produce an animated film of his own, independently of Cosgrove Hall. The idea had been sparked by Pete Garner who he had met up with again in Paperchase. Between them, they wrote a short script and Squire produced the models before they shelved the project to get back into music.

While Couzens was between bands again, he noticed that the musical scene in Britain was changing around him. He took the opportunity to try and broaden his own already eclectic tastes.

"I remember starting getting into The Misunderstood and stuff like that," he said.

The Misunderstood were a throwback to the 1960s. They were a five-piece band, formed in San Francisco during the summer of 1965, who wrote their own distinct brand of hard-edged psychedelic songs. However, they were overshadowed by other west coast bands, such as The Grateful Dead, Jefferson Airplane, and Big Brother and the Holding Company. Frustrated by their lack of progress in the US, their British guitarist persuaded them to try their luck in England. The Misunderstood arrived in the UK in mid-1966 and their talents were quickly recognized. Immediately the group secured a recording contract with Fontana Records, becoming label mates with The High Numbers, who later renamed themselves The Who. The Misunderstood went into the studio in the early part of November 1966 and recorded six singles. This would mark the first and last time the band would ever record with its original line-up. The following month, their first single was released. It was a self-penned number titled "I Can Take You To The Sun" with "Who Do You Love" on the B side. Unfortunately, the band could not have picked a worse time to bring their debut single to the market. At the same time as The Misunderstood attempted to catch the ear of the record-buying public in the UK, the Jimi Hendrix Experience exploded onto the scene with the release of their first disc, "Hey Joe." Just as hopes for some much-needed airplay for the single revived, the band were pushed back into the shadows when, two months later, the Beatles released "Strawberry Fields Forever." However, many connoisseurs of the era still rate "I Can Take You To The Sun" as one of the best psychedelic songs of the 1960s.

Their next single, recorded at the same sessions in November 1966, was "Children Of The Sun" backed with "I Unseen." Inexplicably, this was not released until March 1969. Both songs were harder rocking numbers characterized by unyielding guitar and drum work, which The Stone Roses would emulate. Amazingly, especially as the single was recorded some two years prior to its release, the single blended in surprisingly well with other hard rock acts and sounds emerging out of the heavy blues influences in England at the time. But this time they had to compete with an emerging Led Zeppelin and the Beatles' *Abbey Road*. Once again The Misunderstood would go unnoticed.

Crucially their final single, "My Mind" backed with "Find The Hidden Door," was never released while the band was in existence. In fact, it first saw the light of day in 1982 as part of an English psychedelic compilation album called *Before The Dream Faded*. In the story of The Stone Roses, it was not just The Misunderstood's sound that was influential, but their archetypal late-Mod image.

"This goes back to the picture on the sleeve of the [Misunderstood] single sleeve the lads gave me when I joined The Patrol," said Couzens. "We wanted that kind of look and I started getting into all that."

In fact, there was not much competition for the band's attention in 1984.

"There never seemed to be much on at the time," Couzens recalled.

All that was to change with the burgeoning of Manchester rave scene, which would soon be characterized by the epithet "Madchester." But things started slowly as Couzens pointed out: "The International opened and loads of those US bands came over."

The International was, in fact, two clubs in the Longsight district of Manchester, one with an entrance on Anson Road, the other with its entrance on adjacent Plymouth Grove. International One, on Anson Road, was a showcase for local talent with a capacity of 800. International Two, on Plymouth Grove, was considerably larger and was a prime venue for major touring bands. International One and Two opened in 1985 and would play a key role in the development of The Stone Roses. The two clubs were owned and run by Gareth Evans, who would become their manager and was instrumental in the creation of *The Stone Roses* album. Beforehand he had let them rehearse daily on stage, which allowed them to perfect their performance and hone their unique sound.

Again Gareth Evans was not a native of Manchester. He was born in the small Welsh town of Cwm, and his family moved to the city when he was 12. His family soon returned to Wales, never really having adjusted to urban life, but Evans was determined to stay: "I was just waiting for my life to begin and I knew it would begin in Manchester," he said.

The teenage Evans, now alone in the city, embraced the Mod scene and began hanging around with scooter boys, even though he never owned his own bike. These scooter gangs were much more violent than those that Ian Brown, John Squire, and Andy Couzens had joined in the early 1980s. Many of their members were deeply involved in crime.

Through this world of violence and crime, Evans, never much of a fighter, developed his own defense mechanism.

"I was one of those who relied on his mouth," said Evans. "I was a very lucky guy. I discovered that you could talk your way out of any situation. I was not tough. I was not a hard guy and, if you could not battle your way out, you had to use verbals."

Evans' entrance into the Manchester music scene came with his job at The Jig Saw club. The then owner of The Jig Saw, David Segde, disappeared, leaving his partner in charge, who in turn left Evans with the job of running the club. The first night that Evans ran the club on his own, the takings were twice what they usually were. From then on, Evans was the sole manager of The Jig Saw club and began to make a reputation for himself as an impresario in Manchester.

Evans hired Roger Eagle as house DJ. Eagle was a prominent figure in the Liverpool punk scene, and was the man who discovered Mick Hucknall of Simply Red fame. Eagle brought The Jig Saw club—and Evans—a respectability that allowed Evans to secure more prestigious acts that would usually not have been seen dead in the dank little basement club.

"It was frustrating," recalled Evans. "I must have taken so many future legends out for something to eat. I just wish I'd known who they were at the time."

Among the big names Evans claimed to have met at the time was Eric Clapton, who he said he took out for a spaghetti bolognese. He also hired a modern jazz combo called Bluesology, which featured a bespectacled pianist named Reginald Dwight. When he went solo, Dwight took the stage name Elton "Hercules" John from the first names of Bluesology's saxophonist Elton Dean and the band's vocalist Long John Baldry,

Eventually Roger Eagle moved on with Gareth Evans to become house DJ at The International. He became an important catalyst in the success of the club. In that capacity, he was also crucial in the development of The Stone Roses, giving them much needed exposure early on in their career.

As well as rubbing shoulders with the soon-to-be celebrity acts that played at The Jig Saw club, Evans also had more seamy connections. The contacts he maintained from the scooter gangs he had been a member of in his youth had now matured into hardened gangsters who ran Manchester's thriving underworld. Though not a gangster himself, his position as a club owner earned him respect with the city's growing criminal element.

Evans had reveled in the Mod scene, not only in Manchester. He also traveled frequently to London to check out the scene there. On one such excursion he caught the attention of Vidal Sassoon, the celebrity hairdresser of the 1960s, and was soon hired as a Mod model in Sassoon's salon. Sassoon also taught Evans how to cut-and-blow-dry. Now with a second string to his bow, Evans started working as a hairdresser back in Manchester.

The rise of David Bowie and his Ziggy Stardust haircuts meant that Evans' skills were in great demand. It did not take long for Evans to open his own hairdressing salon. Soon he was joint owner of a chain of over 30 hairdressers in the Manchester area called Gareth And Colin Crimpers. This would make him influential in The Stone Roses' styling and general Mod outlook. They would also benefit from his business acumen. At its height, Gareth And Colin Crimpers even had a branch in Düsseldorf, West Germany.

The international success of the hairdressing chain lead to another enterprise called Salon Masterplan where Evans would outfit new hairdressers across the north-west. Evans then moved into other areas of business. He briefly got into sports retail before turning his attention to trading in gold bullion. He started a company called Gold Inc. with his girlfriend Page Taylor and would travel to London and trade gold, returning with vast sums of cash. Unfortunately, this came to the attention of the Manchester underworld. The British police got word that he was the target for a "hit." He was warned of the danger via the public address system on the train. It seemed like a good time for Evans to get out of the bullion business.

Ever the entrepreneur, he turned his attentions back to club management, making himself central to Manchester's flourishing music scene. He bought an old club, called Oceans 11—named after the classic 1960s' Las Vegas crime-caper movie starring Frank Sinatra, Dean Martin, and Sammy Davis Jnr, recently remade with George Clooney, Brad Pitt, Matt Damon, and Julia Roberts. If that name was not glamorous enough, Evans set horizons even wider and renamed the club The International. Evans re-recruited Roger Eagle and began importing breaking acts from the United States. However, not everyone approved of the direction the International was taking.

"I remember it started having bands like Jason And The Scorchers, loads of stuff from the States," said Couzens. "I went and they were crap—all rubbish. I hate all that Yank shit anyway."

There was little light to break the bleak northern gloom, as Couzens explained: "The London band Brigandage showed a bit of promise, but fell apart on their faces. It was a really horrible period, nothing seemed to be happening. Manchester was really horrible then. It was shite."

Couzens was still hanging out with the lads from The Waterfront after the band had broken up, even though it was a long commute from his parents' home in Macclesfield.

"I still saw Kaiser, Chris Goodwin, and Mani," he said. "I remember us having fights in Piccadilly Gardens and fights with beer monsters waiting for buses. I do remember John getting his nose broken a lot. Ha, ha. One night we were coming out of Club Tropicana on Oxford Road—the one with the palm trees inside—and we got a right hiding. We used to go to [the club] Berlin a lot. Our first demo as the Roses got played in there one night just after we finished it, which was a shock."

The one band member missing from these lads' nights out was Ian Brown. He would rarely come out with the others as he was in an intense relationship with his girlfriend Mitch, who had moved in with him. But Couzens would often go around to their apartment in Hulme as it was on his way home to Macclesfield.

"I'd go around to Ian's quite a lot anyway," said Couzens. "He was living with Mitch, the mother of his children. She had been at college with us in South Trafford and she was working on *Brookside*."

Brookside—commonly known as *Brookie*—was a UK soap opera set in Liverpool, which ran through the 1980s and 1990s.

With his long-term girlfriend, Brown had retreated into a very domestic existence. Music was no longer part of his life. Rather, he was into cookery.

"All I remember is his wok," recalled Couzens. "He loved his wok. He fancied himself as a bit of a cook."

But Couzens was desperate to form a band again. While the other former members of The Waterfront were getting on with their lives, he was drifting around town getting in trouble because of the violent temper that had attracted the other members of the band to him in the first place, and had eventually got him kicked out of college.

"I had all that shit from fighting again," he said. "I have one of those temperaments. Some people have a short fuse; I don't have a fuse at all—bang and I'm gone. I just kept getting in trouble like that. I needed something. I had a court case coming up for fighting." He went to see Brown. "I was hoping he wanted to make some music again. I was keeping my fingers crossed. I said let's get something going, because if I don't I am going to go down. I was staring at a jail sentence. They told me I was going to get six months."

Couzens was scared to death of winding up in prison and knew that the energy he expended being in a band would help keep him out of trouble. He also knew that if he could convince Brown to join him in a new band, Squire and rest would follow suit. He did his best to persuade Brown to join, but Brown had his apprehensions.

"I'd given up rock 'n' roll in one sense," recalled Brown.

However, it did not take long for Couzens to talk him around. After his meeting with Geno Washington, music seemed to promise a way ahead. Couzens finally won Brown over and the two of them began discussing who else they should approach.

"So I was there with Ian in Hulme," he explained. "I was saying 'right, let's get something going again.' We talked about it a bit, what the line-up should be."

Even though it was initially Couzens' idea to reform the band, Ian Brown took over the task of recruiting. Brown knew that they would need Squire if they were ever going to do anything serious. Squire was the master musician and the only one really capable of writing songs at that point, although Couzens was concerned that Squire might not be enthusiastic to join a band he had not started himself. But Brown knew that he would have to persuade Squire no matter what. In the end Squire did not take much persuading at all, as Brown recalled: "There wasn't much else happening. Manchester was so dull at that point and it didn't take long for me and Andy to start getting excited again. A lot depended on how John would react. He was the only one who really knew what he was doing musically. And when we asked him it was so obvious that he was looking to do some thing musical that he agreed immediately."

With Squire now back in the fold, they got to work on the rest of the line-up.

"I wanted Si Wolstencroft, and I know we were thinking of bass players, but who could we get?" said Couzens.

Brown rang around and got in touch with Wolstencroft. Wolstencroft was not doing much at the time as Andy Rourke and Johnny Marr had now left Freaky Party to form The Smiths, so Wolstencroft jumped at the chance to come back in.

Unfortunately, Mani was not available because he was involved in some project of his own in north Manchester, although they kept in touch with him and still hoped to be able to recruit him at some stage, as Couzens recalled: "Mani was someone you went out and had a laugh with, but he was in that Failsworth gang."

With Mani occupied elsewhere, they decided to see if they could reform with the original Patrol line up. So Brown and Couzens' thoughts turned back to Pete Garner.

"We liked Pete," said Couzens. "I always thought there was something about Pete. He's a great bloke, Pete, someone who is great to have around. Whether he could play or not was irrelevant. The fact was he was great to have around, which added to the whole thing."

Squire approached Garner and told him about the new band they were forming.

"At the time, just before, we started I didn't see a lot of Ian and Andy. They were all into scooters," said Garner. "John said that he'd spoken to Ian who had said he wanted to get something together again, and did I want to play bass?"

Thanks to their independent animation project, Garner and Squire had been keeping in regular contact and he jumped at the chance. Now everyone was back in place.

"With John on board, it just felt right," said Couzens. "We ended up getting The Patrol back together. With the big reformation in 1983, in fact, The Roses started to get together."

The original line up of The Stone Roses was now set, although they were not called The Stone Roses. That would come later.

"The first rehearsal was at my parents' house," Couzens recalled. "We actually wrote a song that first night. It was 'Nowhere Fast.' It had another title at the time. I can't remember what the name was now. John had a bit of a riff. He had the opening riff and the chorus and I had couple of parts. Si started drumming and it came together. Not a bad start. We just worked on new stuff, no Patrol or Waterfront stuff. It was a total clean break."

This new band developed quickly, in spite of the fact that Garner couldn't really play bass at all. In fact, he knew less about bass playing than Ian Brown had when he had played bass in The Patrol. He later recalled, with some embarrassment, how far behind the others he was in terms of musical ability: "You've got to remember that the only bass line I knew was 'Blockbuster' from that Patrol gig years ago. I couldn't play the bass at all. I had only played once at that gig. At our first rehearsal everyone strapped on guitars and I was stood there saying, 'what the fuck do I do!'"

Garner certainly had a baptism of fire. The band's progress was swift and by the end of that first week they extended their catalog to three songs.

Brown had problems too. He certainly had the charisma to be lead singer, and could carry a tune, but his voice was a little drab. So he decided to take a few singing lessons. He went to a singing tutor called Mrs. Rhodes, who had a place near Victoria Station in the center of Manchester. There he began to hone his voice. Of course, in rock 'n' roll, taking singing lessons is considered beyond the pale, but Brown was determined, and his karate practice had taught him about the value of discipline.

"We started a few rehearsals and I'm singing and everyone's like, fuck, we can't put up with that! You'll have to have singing lessons," explained Brown. "So I went to this old woman over Victoria Station, Mrs. Rhodes. She'd get me there at six o'clock, open the window. With everyone coming home from work, she'd have me wailing 'After The Gold Rush' or 'Strawberry Fields' out of the window. The crowd's looking up and she's saying if you can't do it, go home. So I thought fuck it, I'll stick it out. So I did three weeks with her. She had an 80-year-old dear on the piano."

It knocked Brown's pride a bit to have to go and get lessons. At school he was never really one who liked to do what he was told. But remembering the Sex Pistols—unbelievably, even Johnny Rotten had had singing lessons—got him through. A lot of critics have since accused Ian Brown of not being able to sing, as he kept quiet about these singing lessons for a long time. However, his voice has since become a template for Britpop singers. But his half-sung voice with its distinct provincial accent was considered a revelation at the time.

With Ian learning how to sing and Pete working out how to play his bass, the band began to come together. A few weeks after they had formed the new band, the songs were developing quickly and they almost had enough material for a full set. Now it was time for them to find a new name for the band.

It was John Squire who came up with the name The Stone Roses. The rest of the band liked the sound of it. They thought it summed them up perfectly.

"We had no name at first, but quickly we were called The Stone Roses," Couzens recalled. "John came up with it. There was a whole list of names written down. Fucked if I can remember them! We had all written loads of stuff down. The Stone Roses was off a book I think, a book cover. The hard and soft thing was an explanation we added later on."

A lot of people have assumed that The Stone Roses was a development from their earlier incarnation as English Rose, but Brown was always quick to dispel this idea: "No, I don't know where that English Rose story came from. John thought up the name Stone Roses—something with a contrast, two words that went against each other."

Now that the band had a name, they would spend a lot of time talking about the sound they were trying to achieve and discussing what influences they should add to the mix. While none of them would deny their punk roots, a lot had happened since the end of The Patrol. They were always very melodic—for a punk band, at least—but since then they each had gone off on differing musical tangents. Wolstencroft brought indie influences with him from his time working with Andy Rourke and Freaky Party. Couzens was interested in the punk-cum-Goth sound that emanated from London.

Goths are an underground British youth movement known for their black clothing, long black hair, wan make-up, black nail varnish on both sexes, facial piercings, and overall Addams Family-cum-Gothic horror-movie look. Musically they are into light metal or "thrash-hop" typified by Type O Negative, the Stone Temple Pilots, Korn, and Rage Against The Machine. The latest exponent is Marilyn Manson.

Garner was still very much into early UK punk, remaining faithful to The Clash, the Sex Pistols, and The Jam. Brown was into Madness and loved ska.

Ska is the generic name for Jamaican music recorded between 1961 and 1967. It exaggerated the "jump" beat heard on the black radio stations from Miami and New Orleans in the 1950s. At that time, most Jamaicans listened to American R&B played on huge over-amplified sound systems. But in the competition between the operators, the owners became record producers. While American R&B mellowed into soul, Jamaican musicians produced a unique hybrid of R&B, doo-wop, and jazz, with a heavy brass element that frequently outshone the vocals. By 1964, ska had become popular among Mods in England, where it became known as Blue Beat, which was the name of the leading UK licensing label. British acts such as Georgie Fame And The Blue Flames and The Migil 5 adopted the ska style, while more authentic Jamaican performers such as the Skatalites, Millie, and Prince Buster had UK hits. By 1966, ska was mellowing into rocksteady, and then reggae, in Jamaica. But its infectious rhythm remained popular in Britain, where there have been several revivals—most notably in the late 1970s/early 1980s when 2 Tone, a conscious mixed-race movement in the English midlands, spawned The Specials and Selecter. Madness, from London's Camden town, had also picked up on ska, adding quirky cockney humor, and witty musical hall lyrics to the mix. They signed to the London punk label, Stiff.

While Ian Brown was getting deeper into the ska scene, Squire was listening to the psychedelic rock of Primal Scream and The Jesus And Mary Chain.

The band The Jesus And Mary Chain were formed in the early 1980s by brothers Jim and William Reid from East Kilbride, a southern suburb of Glasgow in Scotland. The brothers were a formidable songwriting duo. William played guitar and Jim provided the vocals. They recruited bassist Douglas Hart and drummer Murray Dalglish. However the latter was quickly replaced in favor of Bobby Gillespie, who later would go on to start the band Primal Scream which Mani would join after the demise of The Stone Roses. The Reids' first album *Psychocandy* was seen as a landmark release. It fused indie guitar rock and 1960s pop. The Jesus And Mary Chain were—and still are—a very influential band in indie circles. They showed that punk rock and industrial music were not necessarily diametrically opposed to pop, and that they could be woven together into music far more than the sum of its parts.

"I loved the sonic action approach to the guitar overdubs and the endless permutations the [Reid] brothers found for those three chords," said Squire. "It changed the way I thought about writing songs."

Gradually The Stone Roses' various musical interests fused through relentless rehearsing. They just practiced over and over in Couzens' basement trying to create and perfect their own unique style out of this mish mash of influences.

"We were listening to old punk stuff," recalled Couzens. "Also I remember Johnny Thunders being a big a thing."

Johnny Thunders, whose real name was Johnny Genzale, was born and brought up in New York. He first came to fame with the band New York Dolls, formed in 1971. The band released two albums, *New York Dolls*, in 1973, and *Too Much Too Soon*, in 1974. These are seen by many as the beginnings of punk rock, thanks mainly to Johnny Thunders' spartan guitar work. The New York Dolls are cited as the foremost influence for the British punk bands of the late 1970s, such as the Sex Pistols, and Johnny Thunders' later solo work also played a vital part in the rise of British punk rock. In 1991, Johnny Thunders was found dead in a hotel room in New Orleans, Louisiana. He had died from alcohol and methadone poisoning.

Adeptly balancing these diverse influences, The Stone Roses felt that they were really getting somewhere and everyone agreed they were finding their musical feet.

According to Couzens: "It just felt good again, you know, it felt right. We just kept writing. All that early stuff like 'Mission Impossible.'"

This became one of their early demo tracks. It was one of the songs where the new drummer Reni first showed his manic ability on the drums. Although "Mission Impossible" did not make *The Stones Roses* album, it became a regular part of their set and was the last track on *Garage Flower*, the album they recorded before *The Stone Roses*, but which was not released until November 1996, after the band had broken up.

"There was also stuff that didn't make it from that period of songs," said Couzens.

When it came picking the material for their live performances—and more so for the album *The Stones Roses*—they were extraordinarily selective. It was their near obsessive perfectionism that made *The Stone Roses* such an outstanding album. It showed a refinement missing from much of the Britpop of that era.

However, it was still not plain sailing for The Stone Roses. Si Wolstencroft had been auditioning for other bands while he was in this early line-up of The Stone Roses. He had worked with a lot of local bands, making him a much bigger name than any of the others on the local music circuit. He had famously turned down the opportunity to work with The Smiths, who were now dominating the Manchester music scene—which itself had become the powerhouse of British pop.

Perhaps because of this missed opportunity, Wolstencroft wanted desperately to work with musicians who were already established. So Wolstencroft quit The Stone Roses after about six months to join The Colourfield, the new band formed by The Specials' front man, Terry Hall.

The Specials had been formed in 1977 in Coventry, a city halfway between London and Manchester in the midlands of England. The flagship band of the 2 Tone label, The Specials were seen as true innovators during the punk era; they began the British ska revival craze of the late 1970s/early 1980s. Their music combined ska's highly danceable jump-up beat with British punk's energy, attitude, and nihilistic political stance. Their biggest UK hit single, "Ghost Town," released in the summer of 1981, was seen as a power condemnation of the social policies of Britain's Conservative government under Margaret Thatcher, who was the UK's prime minister from 1979 to 1990. Her version of "Reaganomics" had lead to soaring unemployment and racial tension in England. Its release coincided with race riots in the predominately black London suburb of Brixton and in Toxteth in Liverpool. In this atmosphere, the single was banned from airplay by the BBC in case it sparked further trouble, but it still went to number one in the UK charts. The Stones Roses were working their musical apprenticeship in this troubled environment.

Losing their drummer was a huge setback for The Stone Roses and they spent the next month or so looking for a replacement. They even tried to rehire Chris Goodwin but he didn't seem to have the commitment.

"We were still at my parents' place," said Couzens. "We got Chris Goodwin in. He came down for one rehearsal and left his kit. It was like he was just looking for somewhere to store it—in my cellar."

Nevertheless they continued working hard, rehearsing relentlessly while searching for another drummer. It was during this time that they wrote "Misery Dictionary," which would become their first single much later. Couzens recalled how they rehearsed and wrote without anyone on drums: "We'd rehearse for ages with no drums at all, which was ridiculous when you think about it. These days you'd get a drum machine."

The important thing was that they were still writing. Their method of composing now, necessarily, concentrated on the guitar.

As Couzens pointed out: "Either me or John would come up with a riff."

But not everything they came up with was successful—at least in the eyes of this small band of perfectionists.

"Couple of songs didn't make it," said Couzens. "I remember mainly the ones we ended up with: 'Mission Impossible,' 'Nowhere Fast'—'Tragic Roundabout' was possibly from around that period as well."

Even though they could still write songs this way, they knew that they were not really a band without a drummer. So they decided for the first time to look farther afield and began auditioning outside their own circle of friends to find one. They put advertisements for a drummer up around town. One was posted on the notice board in the musical equipment store A1 Music. The first reply was from Howard Daniels, a Manchester-based drummer who had played with the Goth-punk band The Skeletal Family from Keighley in the neighboring county of West Yorkshire.

"We started auditioning drummers," recalled Couzens. "We put an advert up in A1 in town. The first person to answer was the ex-drummer from The Skeletal Family. He came down in his ginger Beetle. You only remember the funny ones, don't you? This guy walked in dressed in leather, a total Goth. He was playing all this tribal stuff—it wasn't right. He kept saying, 'I can't hear the tune.' He didn't seem to be enjoying himself so he didn't get the job."

All The Stone Roses could do was keep auditioning and wait for the right person to come along. Fortunately they did not have to wait too long. A few days after, they had put a second advertisement on the A1 notice board. They soon got the call from a strange-looking young lad named Reni.

Alan "Reni" Wren was born on April 10, 1964. His parents owned a pub in Gorton, east central Manchester. The family lived above the pub. They had a drum kit set up in the corner of the bar for the live bands that played there to use. From an early age Reni would muck about on this old drum kit. As far as Pete Garner was concerned, this gave him an impressive résumé: "Reni's mum and dad ran a pub and they had a drum kit set up for bands in the pub. After school he would come home and play on the kit."

By his teenage years Reni had developed into an accomplished drummer, often sitting in with the pub bands that would pass through his parents' saloon bar. Then he joined a couple of local bands, including the rock outfit, Tora, Tora, in which, it is said, he replaced his best friend and fellow drummer, Simon Wright. On a summer's day in 1984, the 20-year-old Reni saw The Stone Roses' ad on the notice board in A1 Music and was convinced that he was the man they were looking for. A few months earlier, Wright had answered an advertisement in a paper, saying, "Drummer wanted, must hit hard and heavy," and found himself miraculously playing for the Australian rock giants AC/DC. Reni knew he was a better drummer than Wright, and now wanted more than anything to be in a successful band. No opportunity was going to pass him by. He tore the advertisement off the notice board so that no one else could beat him to the punch, then he sped from A1 Music for home, dialed the number and booked himself an audition.

Andy Couzens remembered the advertisement well: "We put an advert in A1 and listed a load of influences, which Reni read but obviously knew none of them."

There was a dispute about what happened next.

"Anyway, Reni rang up," said Couzens. "He denies it now, but he called himself Renée on the phone."

Despite what was taken to be a dangerous sign of pretentiousness, The Stone Roses thought they ought to check out this new drummer.

"Me and Ian went to pick him up, we knocked on his door in Gorton. He came to the door. I seem to remember he looked mad. He had a big long coat on with these big furry moon boots, and a pair of them awful stretch denim jeans. His dress sense was fucking terrible," said Couzens.

By this time, The Stone Roses had become more serious about their music. They had now got some money together to hire some proper rehearsal rooms. On May 31, 1984, they took a room in Decibel Studios in the center of Manchester where they held Reni's audition.

"We loaded his gear into the car and went to the rehearsal room," continued Couzens. "We took the gear up three flights of stairs. It was such a pain in the ass."

But it would be worth it. Reni sauntered into the rehearsal room and set up his gear. Then the band asked him to play the first song that they had written under the name of The Stone Roses, "Nowhere Fast."

"When he started playing he was mad as a hatter," Couzens recalled. "He played like Keith Moon [The Who's legendary drummer]."

At their first gig at The Moonlight Club in north London six months later, The Who's guitarist Pete Townshend made the same comparison, saying that Reni was the best drummer he'd seen since Keith Moon. Moon had died from an overdose of sedatives six years before.

On top of the manic Moon-like energy of Reni's drumming, Couzens was impressed by his extraordinary technical ability: "All those little things that he can do— double hits, unbelievable stuff. So fluent, no effort. He can actually do all that. Amazing. We wanted him in straight away he was that fucking good."

Garner also remembered the impact Reni had on the band when he picked up a pair of drumsticks. They were so impressed that the audition rapidly turned into a full-scale band rehearsal.

"'Nowhere Fast,' 'All Stitched Up,' 'I Can't Take It Anymore,' 'Mission Impossible' were the songs that Reni first rehearsed," said Garner.

There was no doubt in anyone's mind that they had found the drummer, at last.

As Garner pointed out: "We never discussed it: we knew he was in. He was fucking amazing. What a drummer! When he joined us he was already in two other bands. He was checking out who was the best bet—I'm not definite about this but he thought we looked interesting. We had something."

But this now presented a new problem. Would such a naturally talented musician want to join a band that had yet to hone its own musical ability to such a dizzying standard?

"We weren't sure if he was going to have it. We weren't that good at all, pretty rough in fact," Couzens admitted.

Reni, too, had his reservations: "When I went to the audition for this lot, I thought they made a horrible racket, but I was struck by their commitment. The whole group were such an oddball collection of long-hairs, scruffs and smoothies that I just had to join in."

In many ways, this first audition-cum-rehearsal with Reni was when The Stones Roses truly came together. With their talented new drummer on board, their live line-up was complete. But Reni had more to offer. Although the band had been writing and developing songs without a drummer for a couple of months, Reni's attacking percussion could drive these tunes along. Now everything seemed to fall into place. The Stone Roses may have already been born, but with the inclusion of Reni they had the creative team who would come up with the unique sound that would be the making of *The Stone Roses*.

Ian Brown later explained how vital the addition of Reni to the line up really was: "Finding Reni was crucial. John was a punk guitarist when we met Reni, but Reni could play anything. He'd been brought up in pubs, so he'd practiced and practiced on his kit and played with proper club entertainers. He had a musical talent that none of the rest of us had. We all had graft and work, but he was born with it."

Even though they now had a settled line-up, there was still a lot to do. The band bid a permanent goodbye to Couzens' out-of-the-way basement in Macclesfield.

"We stayed in town," said Couzens.

The Roses were a serious Manchester band now and Decibel Studios became their main rehearsal space. They rehearsed there throughout the summer of 1984, though Brown took off briefly on one of his backpacking jaunts on the continent.

There was a downside to the move to Decibel Studios. Their equipment had been safe in the basement of Couzen's parents' house. The rehearsal rooms at Decibel were not nearly as secure. They soon became fed up with the place when some of their equipment went missing. It has to be said that they never liked the ill-maintained Decibel Studios in the first place, so they moved to a plusher, more high-tech studio, with carpeted corridors and larger rehearsal rooms, nearby.

"We rehearsed in Decibel for a good while and then we went to Out Of The Blue fleetingly and then onto Spirit Studios, which became our base for a long time," said Couzens.

The addition of Reni and the move gave the band a renewed burst of creativity.

"When someone joins and you get a new rehearsal room then loads of material seems to get written," Couzens recalled. "In Decibel the songs we put together were 'Mission Impossible' and 'Nowhere Fast.' In Spirit the songs we started getting together were 'Tragic Roundabout,' 'So Young,' 'Tell Me,' and 'Fall.'"

While the move to Decibel gave them the tracks for their first demo, the move to Spirit marked their transition from punk to pop. All these tracks would end up on their 1996 album, *Garage Flower*, with "Nowhere Fast" retitled "Just A Little Bit." The track "So Young" had formerly been titled "Misery Dictionary."

Spirit Studios were run by Steve Atherton (a.k.a. Steve Adge) who would later play a crucial part in the story of The Stone Roses. Andy Couzens recalled his first impressions of Steve: "Spirit was where we met Steve Adge—another nutter, we always seemed to attract them. He was a lot older than us, we were in our early twenties, and he was in his thirties. He was from Hyde and they are a bit strange out there."

Hyde is a suburb on the most easterly outskirts of Manchester, bordering on the hills and moors of the Peak District National Park.

Adge really liked what The Stone Roses were doing in the rehearsal rooms. Running a studio, he had heard a lot of young bands, and he could see genuine potential in The Roses.

Spirit studios themselves were split between two locations. One was in Tariff Road in the city center a few blocks from Decibel. The other was out in the suburbs of Chorlton in east Manchester. This worked to the band's advantage.

"If you dry up, then go to a new room and start again," said Couzens. "The songs will come."

According to Couzens, moving between these different rooms boosted the band's creativity and The Stone Roses shuttled back and forth between the city center and the suburbs. The early tracks had been written in the downtown rooms.

"Then we went out to Chorlton and wrote 'I Wanna Be Adored,'" Couzens remembered.

This was the first song they had written that would appear on the album *The Stone Roses*.

"We also wrote 'Here It Comes' there as well," said Couzens.

This became the B side of "Sally Cinnamon," their second single.

As the band developed musically, Garner's limitations on the bass became apparent. Couzens and Squire had to cover for him during compositional sessions in the rehearsal rooms.

"By this time Pete used to sit out a bit," Couzens pointed out, "and I'd play the bass while we jammed basic things out, then give the bass back and show him what I had been playing. Likewise John would do the same."

They worked hard all summer, commuting between the rehearsal rooms. As the summer drew to a close, The Stone Roses recorded their first demo. They went into the studio on August 26, 1984. The four songs that they decided to record on the demo were "Misery Dictionary," "Mission Impossible," "Nowhere Fast," and "Tragic Roundabout." By that time Reni had been with them for three months. It was this demo that would wind up being played in the Berlin club, the night after they finished recording it in Spirit Studios. They were pleased with the results.

"It sounds better than the Hannett album we recorded later on," recalled Garner.

Martin Hannett was the producer that The Stones Roses went to when they wanted to make their first album. This should have been their début album, but it was only released much later, long after The Roses had disbanded, as *Garage Flower*.

"The demo was a lot more raw," said Garner. "You can hear Reni's drums. I never thought that Hannett suited the band.

Listen to our earlier stuff. This is what we really sounded like. Reni never played the same thing twice, which was pretty mental when it came to recording."

It was during the recording of this demo that the band changed the name of "Misery Dictionary" to "So Young." They did this because the title might have lead people to believe that they had been overly influenced by The Smiths. It is popularly supposed that The Stone Roses despised The Smiths. In fact, they were simply indifferent to them.

"I like the fact that The Smiths came from our home town," said Brown, "and I knew Andy Rourke [The Smiths' early bass player] when I was a kid, so I was happy for them. I liked 'What Difference Does It Make?' But after that, no, not really."

Andy Couzens also dispelled the myth that The Stone Roses harbored any envy or hatred for The Smiths: "We had this song, 'Boy On A Pedestal'—it was very Smithsy, both the title and the lyric. We sort of hated them, but had a secret adoration of them as well."

This track was never released.

The Stone Roses produced 100 cassette copies of their first demo. Squire designed the cover, a thing he would do with all The Stone Roses' singles and albums until he left the band 12 years later. Now they had made their first tentative steps towards a recording career, it was time for the band to start gigging.

Garner recalled how their first gig came about: "We'd buy *Sounds* magazine every week, and Ian noticed an advert for a benefit gig in London with an address to send a demo and Ian, being the main hustler in the band, phones up and sends a tape to this woman called Caroline Reed who was promoting the show at the Moonlight. We didn't really expect to get a reply, but Ian told her we were massive in Manchester. I guess that must have swung it."

Little did anyone realize that Ian Brown's mendacity on the phone to Caroline Reed would become a self-fulfilling prophecy.

Brown recalled how his sheer *chutzpah* paid dividends: "The first Roses gig was at the Moonlight in Hampstead. It was an anti-heroin benefit that Pete Townshend put on. I'd seen an advert in the paper saying they were looking for bands. I lived in Hulme, where everyone was on heroin except for me. So I wrote a letter saying I'm surrounded by skagheads, I want to smash them. Can you give us a show? And they did."

Brown was wrong. It was not his barefaced audacity that won the day. It was the quality of the work on the demo he had sent that won them the gig. As well as signing the acts for the anti-heroin benefit, Caroline Reed was the head of Before The Storm Management. One of her own company's bands, Mercenary Skank, were due to play at the gig and their lead guitarist Andrew Tunnicliffe also helped with managerial duties.

"Being management we'd get the odd tape," said Tunnicliffe. "The management was part of the band as well."

Consequently, he was one of the first outside Manchester to hear The Stone Roses' demo.

"The first impression we got of them was when they sent our management company a demo tape," commented Tunnicliffe. "We thought it was fantastic. We played it all the time. At the time there was no one we really liked. The Stone Roses sounded like they had the same kind of bloodline, like

The Clash and the Pistols and stuff like that. It was a really good tape. I remember 'So Young' being really good."

Before The Storm Management were eager to meet the young turks from the north.

"So Caroline contacted them and they came down to meet us in Hammersmith," recalled Tunnicliffe. "It was way before the gig."

A few weeks later, in late September, Couzens drove the band down to London to meet with Caroline Reed and Mercenary Skank. The meeting was abrasive.

"They all came down and they had a surly, shitty attitude," said Tunnicliffe, "which we liked. They seemed to like to do things en masse. Just taking the piss all the time, anti everything like young bands should be. We said that we liked them so much that we would like to help them."

During this meeting, Caroline Reed agreed to manage the band in London, even though this agreement was never official. She secured them their first gig and lined up two other gigs for them afterward.

"Caroline wanted to sign them to her company—Before The Storm Management," said Tunnicliffe. "She asked them to do gigs with us. They did the anti-heroin benefit with us at the Moonlight Club in West Hampstead. They seemed pretty keen to get involved."

Pete Garner also recalled the trip to London and their aggressive behavior at the meeting with Caroline Reed and Andrew Tunnicliffe: "So we went down to London before the Moonlight gig—the whole band, everyone went to everything. Loads of people said we seemed aggressive at the time. I didn't see it as aggression as I was in the bubble."

This surly behavior became a trademark of the band.

"People said they were intimidated by us," Garner continued. "They assumed everyone in the band was a wanker [jerk-off] because we were pretty arrogant about it."

This arrogance sprang directly from The Stone Roses' own view of themselves. Although The Stones Roses have since come to represent the Manchester—or Madchester—music scene of the late 1980s, they saw themselves as outsiders and far removed from everything that was going on in their home town. They did not want to be seen as just another young band from Manchester and it is clear that they made a conscious effort to do their first gig outside of Manchester. With England's acrimonious north-south divide, to make their stage debut in London was practically treason. This plainly showed how much distance they wanted to put between them and their roots. They already knew that they were destined to become an international phenomenon.

"We didn't want anything to do with Manchester at all," said Couzens. "We opposed all the raincoat-wearing Manchester Factory bands with all their cliquey elitism."

With "Pretty Girls Make Graves," "Heaven Knows I'm Miserable Now," and other angst-ridden tracks, The Smiths, for example, were in full pseudo-intellectual mode. Indeed, The Stone Roses' song "Fall" called for the destruction of the Hacienda and Factory Records.

After the meeting with Reed and Tunnicliffe, The Stone Roses went back to Manchester for a month. During that time and up until their scheduled performamce in West Hampstead in October, they made no effort to play outside the rehearsal rooms. But they were brimming with

The Stone Roses: (clockwise from the top) Mani (Gary Mountfield), Ian Brown, John Squire, and Reni (Alan Wren).

On the verge of the band's first big break-through, Stone Roses vocalist Ian Brown in a 1988 studio photo.

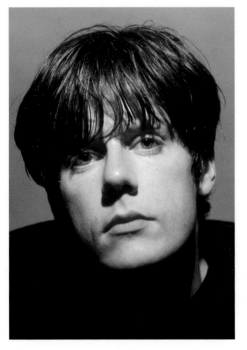

Guitarist John Squire, along with Ian Brown a founder member of the 'Roses, who he would eventually leave in 1996.

*Mani in September
1988, a year after
he'd replaced founder
member Pete Garner
on bass guitar.*

*Drummer Reni: also a
member of the 'Roses
original five-piece
line-up along with
Brown, Squire, Pete
Garner, and guitarist
Andy Couzens.*

The Roses on television, from the local Granada Stdios in their native Manchester, January 1989.

Ian Brown gives it his all during a concert appearance on tour in Japan in 1995.

The now-legendary Stone Roses gig at Spike Island in Widnes, Cheshire, on May 27 1990.

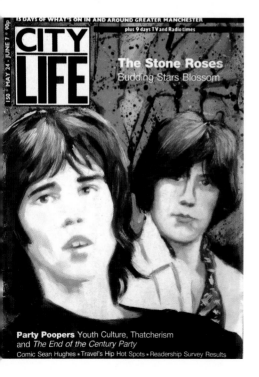

The Stone Roses
made the front cover
of Manchester's
leading what's-on
magazine City Life
in May 1990.

The Roses first manager Howard Jones, also manager of the Hacienda Club in Manchester at the time, seen here in his office in 1985.

Manchester rock scene main man Anthony Wilson, founder and proprietor of the influential Factory Records label.

The Stone Roses contemporaries on the "Madchester" scene, Happy Mondays, in April 1987.

Stone Roses manager Gareth Evans (left) at the Spike Island concert with Happy Mondays vocalist Shaun Ryder.

Happy days: Ian Brown in the foreground as the Stone Roses enjoy the sun before their eventual demise in 1996.

confidence. Even though The Stone Roses had been rehearsing and writing all summer, now that they finally had a gig, they felt they could call themselves a proper band.

When finally October 23, 1984—the day of the gig—arrived, Kaiser drove the band down to London.

"When the Roses started I used to help them out," said Kaiser. "I would drive the van and help set the gear up."

The former Waterfront lead singer had now become The Stone Roses' casual roadie. He was pleased that his former band mates were having success as The Stone Roses and bore them no ill will.

On the long trip down the motorway to London, the band were very excited. Ironically, as they were playing an anti-drugs benefit, they began taking lots of amphetamines.

"That time they played the first gig," recalled Kaiser, "the anti-drugs gig, they were all out of their heads speeding. But then the Roses, like most of the punk generation, didn't look on speed as a drug. Smack and dope were drugs—hippie shit. Speed made you think fierce. Made you more aware, crazier. It was sharp and dangerous. It didn't mong you out [damage your brain]—well, not for a few years anyway."

Ian Brown recalled the state they were in when The Stone Roses finally made it onto the stage for their first performance: "When we played the anti-heroin benefit, we went on speeding out of our minds." But Brown refused to see the irony of this.

"No, we are anti-drugs," he said, "except for speed and cannabis, that is."

So the band arrived for the sound-check, high on speed and adrenaline. They set their gear up and did a quick warm-up. They found themselves playing so well that they even impressed the other bands.

"That first gig at the Moonlight, in the sound-check the song that we did was 'Open Your Eyes' by The Nazz," said Garner. The Nazz were a Philadelphia-based, anglophile rock/pop quartet formed in the late 1960s. "The version we did was really tough. It's a great song live, really good and people were going: 'Fucking hell!'"

Reni's drumming particularly impressed.

"We'd do sound-checks and Reni had people with their mouths open," said Brown.

"People were coming up and saying where are you from?" Garner recalled. "We had had so much whiz [anphetamine] by this point, that everything was very intense. We were doing loads of speed that night. In those days we were massively into speed—that was the main thing for us. We took it religiously. The only person who never did any speed was Reni, but he was such a natural speed head that he didn't need any."

Before The Storm Management were not disappointed by their new discovery. The Stone Roses' performance blew them away.

As Tunnicliffe stated: "They were great on stage."

If the band were good that night bolstered by speed, then Reni, without it, was exceptional. Pete Garner recalled how outstanding Reni's playing was.

That night, again, Garner said: "Reni never played the same thing twice."

The band did though, in the set, as well as in the sound-check, they played The Nazz's "Open Your Eyes." This did not bother Reni though.

"You would do a song and five minutes later when you played it again, he played it completely differently," said Garner. "He was amazing. It was like having ten Keith Moons playing all at once."

The gig at the Moonlight was unique as it was the only time The Stone Roses played the only full cover version of someone else's song—their version of The Nazz's "Open Your Eyes."

"Me and John were mad on The Nazz," explained Garner. "It was one of our favorite groups at the time. Pete Townshend told us we reminded him of the early Who so we had hard-ons all the way home."

Having been a speed freak in his early days with The Who, Pete Townshend was very much in tune with the band.

"It's great to see five arrogant kids on stage," he said.

The early Who, the great Mod band of their day, were also known in the 1960s for their arrogance. In their case, as in that of The Stone Roses, it was both justified and paid off.

Reni even got to play a reincarnation of Keith Moon that night. Townshend was planning to close the show with a few tunes of his own and asked Reni if he could play the drums for him. The Mercenary Skank guitarist Andrew Tunnicliffe also played with Townshend that night.

"Pete Townshend was particularly impressed with Reni and asked him to get up for 'Substitute' and 'Pictures Of Lily,'" said Tunnicliffe.

Ian Brown recalled the circumstances: "We had come off stage and Townshend was like, 'You look really good up there and your drummer's great,' then he said, as an end-of-the-night thing, I want to play a couple of tunes. Do you want to do it? Reni's like, 'Yeah!'"

Brown looked on in awe: "Reni did 'Pictures Of Lily' and 'Substitute' with Pete Townshend. He was made up—his first-ever gig and there he was with Pete Townshend."

Andy Couzens' account of these events was more caustic. He recalled the band had little time for the likes of Pete Townshend: "We just said to him, 'Who the fuck are you?' Everyone had a colossal ego in the band. That was our attitude at the time. He had asked if he could borrow our drummer and we just pointed to this heap on the floor. I remember at the end of the set at those times Reni would collapse onto the floor. It was hard to tell whether he was putting it on or not, although he put so much into it, it could have conceivably been true. We said to Townshend, 'If you want him he's over there, just go and ask him.'"

Pete Garner remembers how Reni responded to Townshend's request.

"As if he was bothered, know what I mean?" said Garner. "He could just drum to anything. He was a total natural. When Pete Townshend asked him to play 'Substitute,' Reni just turned to him and yelled, 'How the fuck does it go?'"

made of stone

The Stone Roses were making rapid progress. They had recorded an impressive demo and had played a prestigious gig with a rock legend who had praised them to the skies— all in the space of three months. But to make an album they needed management. Caroline Reed and Before The Storm Management, though helpful, were in London—too far away to be of much assistance.

Help came from an unlikely source. Howard Jones—the former general manager of the Hacienda and, hence, one of the enemy—became The Stone Roses' first full-time manager. He had come into contact with the band through Steve Adge from Spirit Studios.

Not only had Howard Jones run the Hacienda, he was the man responsible for opening it. But after two years of managing the most famous nightclub in Manchester, Jones now felt constricted.

The Factory label that dominated Manchester music at the time owned the Hacienda and supplied acts for the club. Jones began to feel that he was a puppet and that they were controlling his every move. He decided to quit and try his hand at managing a band. He wanted to show Factory that he could make it under his own steam. The challenge was to find a good band and take them to the top.

Around the time that The Stones Roses were doing their first gig in London, Jones was scouring the Manchester rehearsal rooms for suitable talent. He got in touch with

Steve Adge and asked if there was anyone at Spirit who the studio manager could recommend.

"Yeah," said Adge, "There's something here you may well be interested in looking at. They're called The Stone Roses."

While Howard Jones was in the process of leaving the Hacienda, Martin Hannett, the leading producer of Factory records, also grew disillusioned with the organization and decided to quit. At the time, Martin Hannett was seen as the premier producer in the Manchester music scene. He had worked with Joy Division and developed a number of other ground-breaking Mancunian acts that were signed to the Factory label.

"By this time I had spent a lot of time recording with Martin Hannett who was also pissed off with Factory," recalled Jones.

When Hannett had worked with Joy Division and New Order, he had pioneered Factory's electronic sound. But, like Jones, he had become frustrated by the restrictions placed on him. He felt that Factory were spending all their money on the loss-making Hacienda, while denying him new equipment and a state-of-the-art studio. It was, after all, the records he produced for them that made them all the money.

Together Hannett and Jones began making plans. They set up a new record label, aiming to rival Factory. It would also be a vehicle for the up-and-coming band Jones intended to manage. Thin Line records was founded on November 12, 1984. Now the label needed a act.

"It had become a bit of a thing for me to find a good band in Manchester," said Jones.

Soon after the founding of Thin Line, Howard Jones got in touch with The Stone Roses and asked them if they would be interested in letting him manage them. He also raised the possibility of signing them to his new record label. It seemed to be too good to be true. The band must have been overwhelmed. As patrons of the Hacienda they knew about Howard Jones and what he could do for them. Indeed, all of Manchester knew the name of Howard Jones. He was a central figure in Manchester's now world-famous music scene. But being The Stone Roses, they played it cool. They could afford to. They already had another two gigs lined up supporting Mercenary Skank on the weekend of November 21–22, thanks to Caroline Reed and Before The Storm Management.

Reed was also trying to get some press coverage together for them. She called a music journalist, named Gary Johnson, who worked for the influential *Sounds* magazine and had seen The Stone Roses play at the Moonlight Club. Johnson tried to get some of his colleagues in the media interested in The Stone Roses and led a press party to their two November shows. The first on November 21 was in Exeter, Devon in south-west England—about as far from Manchester as you can get. The show the following day was at the Ad Lib Club in Kensington, an up-market district of London. Although Mercenary Skank played at both gigs, their guitarist Andrew Tunnicliffe only recalled the first performance: "I'm sure the only other gig we played with them was Exeter Labour Club, I can't remember the London show at all."

Despite his lapse of memory, he did remember that, in Exeter, The Stone Roses even outstripped their performance at the Moonlight Club.

"They were great, even better the second time," said Tunnicliffe. "The guitars were full on. They went on stage and made a racket. I particularly liked them. They really reminded me of early Clash. For some reason I remember John Squire having some sort of flares on. He always had his distortion pedal full on. I tried to tell him he didn't have to do that. Andy and Ian Brown would career around the stage. They also had a very glam, longhaired Gothy type in the band as well." This was Pete Garner.

Tunnicliffe also remembered that they went down well with the West Country audience.

"Whoever turned up at the gigs really liked them as well," he said.

However, although they were well received, by Tunnicliffe at least, the gig was not well attended. Only about 40 people turned up and, according to some sources, they could scarcely believe their eyes.

Tunnicliffe was also surprised to find that The Stone Roses' behavior did not live up to their bad-boy image.

As he recalled: "They might have had an attitude but they were really nice people as well, polite even. Their attitude reminded me of what we were like when we started in the punk days."

At the Ad Lib Club back in London the next night, The Stone Roses played what eyewitnesses said was their best gig yet. Thanks to Caroline Reed, the gig earned The Stone Roses their first review. It was in their favorite magazine, *Sounds*. But it was not by Gary Johnson, who had been championing the band. The review was written by another journalist, Robin Gibson, who savaged The Stone Roses and their performance. The band were not perturbed by this bad review. Although new to the business, The Stone Roses already knew that in pop and rock there is no such thing as bad press—especially when it is in a national publication.

Meanwhile Howard Jones was being very patient. He waited until after The Stone Roses had performed their two support spots with Mercenary Skank, then arranged to go and hear them when they returned to Manchester.

Jones and The Stone Roses finally got together at Spirit Studios, on November 29, 1984. He recalled his first impressions of the band: "I went down to Spirit to check out the Roses, and they were absolutely fucking diabolical. It was a racket, but one of those kinds of rackets that are so exciting. They had songs there."

He was particularly impressed by the lyrics.

"I couldn't believe some of the lyrical content," said Jones. "It was brilliant. I'm well into lyrics—I love Dylan—and Ian Brown's lyrics were great."

He found the enigmatic Brown especially intriguing: "I was thinking: Does Ian realize how evocative his words are? They work on so many levels. Does he understand how powerful these words are?"

As a personal and professional relationship developed between the members of the band and their new manager, Jones realized that Brown was, indeed, master of his craft. He was fully aware how evocative and powerful some of his lyrics were.

"I eventually got to know Ian and got to realize how deep a thinker he really is," said Jones. "There isn't a thing he doesn't think about. I thought this guy is a great songwriter."

But it wasn't just Ian Brown's lyrics that appealed to Howard Jones. He liked The Stone Roses' appearance too. "They looked great," said Jones, "like a gang, each one different. Like a tall one, a thin one, a hard one, a soft-looking one, and John looked like if you said boo he would jump. Reni looked so young, I didn't realize he was so young, I couldn't believe it."

But Reni's drumming could not fail to amaze.

"Reni was the most brilliant drummer I had ever seen or have ever seen since," Jones recalled. "When he got behind a kit, the kit became an extension of him in the same way Hendrix's guitar would be."

Although impressed, Jones was not 100 percent sure that The Stone Roses were the band that he wanted to launch his record label with. But he knew that he could not waste any time in coming to a decision and realized that he had to follow his feelings.

"Everything is about instinct. I had heard a lot of bands that were better then them and more ready musically but I thought, this band has got legs. This will go," he said.

Couzens recalled that they were making a bit of a racket the day Jones first visited Spirit: "Howard said the same thing—that we made this racket. He couldn't make out the songs because it was so loud and distorted, but there was something in the self-belief and conviction that made him think, 'Yeah, these are great.'"

Jones was brimming with confidence.

"I was full of it anyway," he said. "I was the big time Hacienda head honcho, Mr. Manchester who didn't pay to get in anywhere."

So Jones decided to sign them. The next day Jones went back to Spirit to talk with the band as they rehearsed. If they agreed to sign with Thin Line, he wanted to get them into the studio with Martin Hannett as soon as possible. But the band still took some convincing.

"They hated the way Hacienda and Factory dominated the Manchester scene," said Jones. "Steve Adge had warned me about this—about how they hated all that scene. They saw me as an insider until I gave them my spiel about how I was nothing to do with Factory any more. I told them that I'm resigning from Factory and starting my own company. I told them that we're going to start a label and the first band I sign will be recorded by Martin Hannett. I said, 'If you go with me now you will have product out within months.'"

That was Howard Jones' pitch and The Stone Roses, despite their affected coolness, knew they would have been stupid not to accept. To have a manager like Jones who had credibility and reputation—plus to be given a chance to record with an established producer and be the first band on a new label—was an offer no ambitious rock band could refuse.

Ian Brown recalled how Howard Jones became their first manager on the strength of the recording deal. In fact, Brown got the impression that Jones and Hannett had set up Thin Line for their benefit: "Howard Jones, the original manager of the Hacienda, who became our manager in 1984, formed a label so that we could release the single, rather than go for a deal [with another company]."

Andy Couzens had a slightly different take on the meeting with Jones that secured him as their manager: "Howard Jones came down, he had just lost his job as general manager of the Hacienda. He said he was setting something up with Martin Hannett."

Jones quickly proved his worth to the band.

"Howard was like having your dad around," said Couzens. "All of a sudden it stopped being a racket. It was a bit more serious."

Jones had distinct ideas about the band, and felt he needed to shape them up. He suggested that Pete Garner cut his hair, which he had been wearing long.

"Your bass player's great, but he needs a hair cut," said Jones.

Garner was not impressed:"I thought, you c**t, and I told him to fuck off. He wasn't happy at all."

But Jones was not to be deterred. He also wanted to radically alter their style of dress. Up until then the band— John Squire in particular—would grace the stage sporting paisley shirts and bandannas. Jones wanted them to leave behind the clichés of rock dress. They needed to look altogether much more cool.

Jones' first act as their manager was to get The Stone Roses to record a new demo. This would be recorded in Spirit Studios by a friend of Jones', named Tim Oliver, and the four tracks that were to be laid down were all new. "Heart On The Staves" later appeared on the *Garage Flower* album. "Going Down" would end up being the B side of their most acclaimed single "Made Of Stone." "The Hardest Thing In The World" would not only be on *Garage Flower* but was also the B side to "Elephant Stone," the first single they made for Zomba Records, which Zomba released on their alternative imprint, the Silvertone label. To these was added "Shoot You

Down," which was the first track they recorded that appears on the album *The Stone Roses*.

The Stone Roses were not happy about being stuck back in Manchester. Their gigs in the Moonlight Club and the Ad Lib had given them a taste for the kind of exposure only the capital could offer and they were reluctant to play on the limited Mancunian circuit.

According to Couzens: "Manchester was a pit, there was nowhere to play. We just thought we may as well concentrate on London. Me and Ian would go down to London and do some hustling as well as the stuff that Caroline Reed sorted for us."

They got a gig in The Greyhound, Fulham, a pub and rock venue in West London, where Jimi Hendrix visited in on his way into London from Heathrow Airport, when he first came to England in 1966.

Meanwhile Howard Jones was hard at work promoting the band in the north. He gave a copy of The Stone Roses' new demo tape to a friend of his named Tony "the Greek" Michaelides, who was a DJ on Piccadilly Radio, Manchester's local music station.

Tony the Greek played the tape on his show *The Last Radio Programme*. The response was overwhelming and immediate.

"People were ringing up," recalled Garner. "It was very rare that people rang up."

The telephone response brought an immediate benefit.

"Then we were booked for a session on the radio," said Garner. "At this point we hadn't even played in Manchester."

Howard Jones was delighted with his own developing managerial prowess: "It was the first live radio session played on Piccadilly Radio for ten years. At first we were going to do it acoustic with just John and Ian, but eventually we decided to do it with the whole band."

In fact, an unplugged session featuring just John Squire and Ian Brown would have evoked huge opposition from the band.

"I've never heard of such a thing," said Garner. "The only person who would have thought of that is Howard. It was never mentioned to us. I mean, why would you do it? It would be a total non-representation of the band, and acoustic version of songs that no one has heard anyway would have been pointless."

This time The Stone Roses did live up to their bad-boy image, but it paid off.

As Garner recalled: "There was some throwing of chairs in the studio—a pretty reckless thing to do, but it gave it an edge. The radio session we did live and it went pretty well."

In these sessions, The Stone Roses played "I Wanna Be Adored" for an audience for the first time. There is now a lucrative market for bootlegs of this Piccadilly radio session. However, Garner maintained that the copies circulating are not, in fact, station recordings of the aired performance. He insisted that the radio sessions were not recorded at all.

"As we were about to take the equipment down and go home, the recording engineer came in and said he forgot to press record," said Garner. "He had put it out live, but hadn't recorded it. We had to do the three songs again and it wasn't half as good. They were repeated quite a few times after that, playing not so good versions, and these are the ones on bootlegs. All the versions I've heard are the shit ones. We'd done our work. Trying to be real for the second time just doesn't work."

Regardless of whether the bootlegs were genuine or not, the Piccadilly Radio session earned The Stone Roses a full page review in the local Manchester music magazine *City Life*. The review may not have exactly sung their praises, but it did not dismiss them either, and again the band considered that there was no such thing as bad press.

After these sessions, on January 19, The Stone Roses appeared at the famous Marquee Club in London's Soho district, where British rock legends, from the Rolling Stones and the Yardbirds, through The Who to the Sex Pistols, made their breakthrough. A fortnight later The Stone Roses played a showcase gig for Piccadilly Radio at the Dingwalls Club in Camden Lock, north London, on February 8, 1985.

Even though Caroline Reed was still working on the band's behalf down in London, they had not told her anything about Howard Jones, and they kept Howard Jones in the dark about Reed.

"I didn't know anything about Caroline Reed," Jones recalled. "What happened was that she thought she was managing them and they never spoke to me about it. She was ringing Andy and he never told me. The first time I met her was four years later when I was going to Berlin with The Buzzcocks. I didn't know anything about Caroline."

The Buzzcocks were another Manchester punk band. Formed in 1975, they gained a cult following in the US after their second tour in 1980. Jones knew them from his time at the Electric Circus.

However, the relationship between The Stone Roses and Caroline Reed soon waned and their opportunities in London dried up. Couzens recalled why this working relationship with Caroline Reed broke down: "Musically Reni was the main strength of the band at the time and she was in total adulation of him. She tried to nick him from us. She wanted him to drum for Mercenary Skank and if she could have got him she would have."

The now fully committed themselves to pursuing their career with Howard Jones and Martin Hannett. After all, it was their chance to start recording seriously—a debut album perhaps? The Stones Roses arranged to start recording with Martin Hannett. They went to Strawberry Studios in nearby Stockport, where Hannett was owed a lot of studio time. Even so, Couzens had to stump up another £1,200 ($1,800) for the recording sessions.

Hannett was said to be the architect of the Factory sound and now The Stone Roses had him to themselves. Given The Stone Roses' anti-Factory stance, this could be regarded as being hypocritical. As the Stones Roses had already been quite vocal about their loathing of the Factory label with "Fall," working with Martin Hannett could be seen as sleeping—or at least recording—with the enemy. However, Martin Hannett had produced another act in his days before Factory—a band that The Stone Roses boys greatly admired—the punk group, Slaughter And The Dogs.

The Stone Roses and Slaughter And The Dogs came from neighboring areas in Manchester. Slaughter came from Wythenshawe, which is just east of The Roses' neighborhood of Altrincham. Brown and Squire were fans of Slaughter And The Dogs back in the days when they attended their high school, Altrincham Grammar School.

"Yeah, I got into them through that single, 'Cranked Up Really High,'" said Brown. "My next door neighbor was a friend of Rossi, the guitarist. I saw them at Wythenshawe Forum and the Belle Vue a few times."

Subsequently, they were a huge influence on the lads when they formed The Patrol.

Hannett may have been a Factory man; on the other hand The Stone Roses found it pretty cool to be working with the producer of the early musical idols. He had been the man on the mixing desk for "Cranked Up Really High." Now The Stone Roses wanted them to produce that same sort of sound for them. They even took a copy of the single into Strawberry Studios, handed it to Hannett, and told him "make us sound like that."

Despite the fact that they were eager to record an album, it was a single that The Stone Roses first worked on with Martin Hannett at Strawberry Studios in March of 1985. The songs they chose to record were "So Young"—formerly "Misery Dictionary"—and "Tell Me." Both tracks appear on *Garage Flower*.

"The single 'So Young' is about when I lived in Hulme," said Brown. "Everyone who lived there seemed to think it was great to stay in bed until tea time. It's just a waste of life. I'm saying you've got to get out of bed today. They could be doing something more worthwhile with their time."

Although Brown was a very personal lyricist, the single reflected the aspirations of the band as a whole and other contemporaries who shared his take on Manchester life.

"It sounds like four lads trying to get out of Manchester," explained Brown. "Mainly the lyrics are about personal experiences, about my friends or how I feel."

Although the band wanted Hannett make them sound like Slaughter And The Dogs, that was not possible. Hannett had worked with Slaughter And The Dogs a long time before he got to work with The Stone Roses, and his time at Factory, working with the likes of Joy Division, had changed his production style too much. Besides, The Stone Roses' own style of music did not really suit Slaughter And The Dogs' out-and-out punk vibe which was now dangerously dated.

However, Martin Hannett's production on The Stone Roses' single captures a muted punk rock feel, while allowing the power of Brown's lyrics to shine through. And The Stone Roses' instinctive feel for melody had begun to soften their hard edge.

Even though the band and Hannett were often at cross-purposes in the studio, The Stone Roses found their time working with him exciting.

As Couzens recalled: "I loved it, even though he was a total mess. He was bad on smack at that point. He kept going on about trying to destroy his ego. But whatever he did, he did it instinctively."

There were other problems. The record was engineered by Chris Nagle, and there was a personality clash between him and Brown.

"Ian just didn't get on with him," said Couzens. "He kept saying that he couldn't get any response from him. So you've got that, and Martin asleep on the couch. It was a weird way to record."

Despite all the communication difficulties that arose while they were working on their first single, their time working with Martin Hannett and Chris Nagle was an educational experience. It was an education that a young band like The Stone Roses was very fortunate to receive and set them in good stead when it came to the recording of the album *The Stone Roses*.

The Piccadilly Radio session had created a fan base for The Stone Roses in their hometown. But their first gig in the north of England was not actually in Manchester but 25 miles away in Preston, a town a little north of Manchester—halfway to the famous seaside resort of Blackpool on the north-west coast. They had been rehearsing hard since the Piccadilly Radio session, fine tuning all of their material, and felt ready to play in front of a critical northern audience—many of whom would make the journey from their hometown. When The Stone Roses played in the Clouds Club on March 29, a huge crowd of people from Manchester made the trip to Preston to see them. Many of them knew the members of The Stone Roses personally and the band took a considerable posse with them.

"I had mates all over town," said Brown, "not just from where I was from, I was hanging with kids everywhere."

The Stone Roses and a hardcore of Manchester music fans invaded Preston that night. Andy Couzens recalled how they descended on Preston en masse: "Steve Adge was the leader of the gang and there were all these punks, Goths and skins from Manchester. Steve loved a rumble and that night with all the tension there was plenty of opportunity for that."

From the beginning there was antagonism between the locals from Preston and The Stone Roses' fans from Manchester.

"It was a really rowdy bunch who came down," said Garner. "All I remember was that when we went to play there, there was tension in the air beforehand with a load of people from another city."

Unfortunately, these tensions coincided with a series of technical problems with the band's equipment. On stage, Couzens' guitar stopped working, then the band's main amp gave up the ghost. Howard Jones tried to rush onto the stage and sort things out, but the band pushed him back into the crowd. Undaunted, Jones tried again. He doggedness earned him a strange nickname among the band.

"That's why we always called him 'The Rhino,'" said Couzens. "We would always give him shit and he would always come back for more."

With or without Jones' help, the technical difficulties resulted in a lengthy period of silence and trouble kicked off in the crowd. There was almost a riot. The band members tried to pacify the audience and just as the atmosphere began to calm down, a string broke on Garner's bass guitar. He then had to spent a minute or so trying to fix it. There was little point as the club descended irretrievably into violence. Garner replaced the string, but in the chaos he was unable to tune the bass. Despite the melee the band tried to soldier on with their set. But Reni lost his temper. He kicked over his drum kit with a crash, Keith Moon-style. Suddenly, The Stone Roses seemed to turn into The Who. Couzens smashed his guitar as if he were Pete Townshend. It was the only one his owned. And the audience joined in this orgy of violence.

Howard Jones recalled the night: "The thing about Ian being a kick boxer is that he can look after himself in those situations. He didn't feel frightened and neither did Andy because Andy is quite 'rough and tumble,' but John and Pete in particular are not fighters and they were terrified."

Garner recalled the Manchester fans fighting with people from Preston: "We went on and it erupted into a Wild West saloon thing. I was glad I wasn't in the audience. It was pretty naughty!"

As the band retreated from the stage, they were approached by Ro Newton, a journalist from the *New Musical Express*. Backstage, she asked them whether they condoned any of the violence that was going on.

"She was trying to get Ian to say, 'Oh yeah, it's a terrible thing,'" said Garner. "But he wouldn't do it, so she went totally against us at that point."

More bad press.

However, the mayhem at the Preston gig brought The Stones Roses a wider reputation. Now people knew who they were. Eventually, after *The Stone Roses* album was released, the *New Musical Express* came round. For the moment though, bad press was a good enough start, but it was not something they capitalized on straight away. Rather than follow up with another UK gig, they were about to go on tour in Sweden. Since the success of Abba, Sweden had become an important country for pop acts to tour. The band played there before ever deciding to show their face in the hometown.

"I don't think we played anywhere in Manchester till after we had been to Sweden," said Couzens.

The Swedish tour came about because Ian Brown had always been a keen traveler, whether it was touring around the coastal towns England on his scooter or backpacking through Europe. During his trip to the continent in the summer of 1984, he had met another backpacker who put him in touch with a Swedish promoter by the name of Andreas Linkaard.

Brown, as always, had talked up The Stone Roses, claiming that his band was huge in England—even though at that time they had yet to play outside the rehearsal room.

"I was in Berlin," said Brown, "and met this kid whose friend was a promoter so I told him we were a big group from Manchester."

They exchanged telephone numbers before Brown returned home to England. Early in 1985, before the disastrous Preston gig, Brown had given the Linkaard contact number to Howard Jones, so that he could arrange some gigs in Sweden. Howard Jones was unsure if this was a wise move for a band in such an early stage of its development. He also doubted that they could live up to the hype Brown had given them.

"I thought it wasn't the best time to go away," recalled Jones. "We were just building up things in Britain and then we would be away for three weeks. I was worried by that."

Nevertheless, Brown was insistent. Jones contacted Linkaard and he set up about eight or nine shows.

They set off just two weeks after the Preston gig. The trip was totally unorganized.

"We literally threw the gear in the back of my big white Chevy truck," said Couzens.

They took a car ferry across the North Sea. It was a long trip, which most passengers spent taking advantage of the low prices in the duty-free bar. Although Brown was a seasoned traveler, foreign travel was a new experience for the rest of the band.

"We knew nothing about customs, we just drove there and got off the boat and drove up to Stockholm," said Couzens.

Reluctant to make the trip in the first place and dealing through contacts that were not his own, Howard Jones let his usually meticulous standard of management slip disastrously and the journey proved shambolic.

"Me, the band, and the roadie—Gluepot Glen—went on the trip," said Jones. "As usual Andy wouldn't let anybody drive his white Chevy—so he drove all the way there. We were all crammed in the back with the gear. Thank God they only had small amps. John and Andy had small Roland amps and we all sat on those. We didn't know what gigs there were, where we were staying, or how much money we were getting."

"We didn't even know how long we were going for when we went," Couzens added.

Jones had not arranged even the simplest things for the trip.

"We arrived in Sweden with no money at all," he said. "We needed some Swedish cash to get petrol. We had got off the ferry in Sweden. We couldn't get petrol. We suddenly realized that there's only £20 [$30] in the kitty."

They were stuck in a blizzard with no petrol. With the engine turned off there was no heat in the truck.

"We could have frozen to death," said Jones. "We sat there in the cold getting colder, hung-over from alcohol. And then in the blizzard a car pulled up. It was the first one in an hour. I jumped out and banged on the window."

The driver, a Swede, opened the window to be confronted with a frantic foreigner.

"Look I've got no money—help," said Jones, in English. "I must have looked like some sort of lunatic mugger appearing out of the snow with a van load of lunatics behind me in the van."

The astonished Swede pulled his wallet out, handed it to Jones, and drove off. The wallet was stuffed with Kronor—the Swedish currency—to the equivalent of $250.

The money was a godsend. They had to drive for 24 hours across the country to Stockholm, the capital of Sweden.

Jones recalled: "We were due to meet Andreas at eight o'clock on April 8 at Stockholm railway station—that was the only plan we had. I often wondered what would have happened if he hadn't been there. We would have been fucked. We didn't have his phone number or anything."

Linkaard was there and eventually took them back to his apartment.

"We got in his [home] at six o'clock Monday morning, and Andy didn't wake up till five o'clock on Tuesday afternoon," Jones added.

The trip to Sweden was to be a formative experience for The Stone Roses. It was first time they would have to live together cheek by jowl, just as they would a few years later when they were recording *The Stone Roses* album.

"We were living in his flat in Stockholm for about a month," said Brown. "It was great." Better still. "We got in the daily papers."

It was also in Sweden that they each committed themselves to the band full time.

"It was our first proper break," said Couzens. "It was where we went serious. We were there for a month, but it seemed like forever."

Even John Squire thought that it was the best time for the band.

"We made John give up his day job," remembered Couzens.

"We got him on the phone in Sweden and made him do it. Ian was signing on [for unemployment benefit] and stopped."

Together in a foreign country, the members of The Stone Roses found a new camaraderie.

For Couzens: "That was where the band first became a proper band and gelled—it was our Hamburg really."

Famously, the Beatles and other important British bands of the 1960s served their musical apprenticeship in the clubs on the Reeperbahn in Hamburg, West Germany.

The Stone Roses' first performance in Sweden was scheduled for April 10. It was at the Big Bang Club in Linköping, a small town 100 miles or so south west of Stockholm. Not only had Andreas Linkaard booked the gig, he had also arranged for The Stone Roses to receive some local press coverage. A large audience waited for the band to come onto the stage. They were patient and well-behaved. It was a huge contrast to Preston.

When Ian Brown opened the show, it was in brash style.

"You're all Swedish twats!" he yelled into the microphone. It was a phrase in Swedish that he had spent many long hours perfecting. This was the beginning of Ian Brown's famed confrontational stage style.

The audience took the insult in good part and the band went down well. And when the crowd called for an encore, The Stone Roses obliged. The Roses would later become infamous for not doing encores. This was a rarity.

The next night they performed at The Olympia Club in Norrköping, 30 miles from Linköping back down the road to Stockholm. After playing in Norrköping they returned to Stockholm. They would have to wait almost two weeks until their next performance date, which was in the capital. Soon they were flat broke. Sweden is a notoriously expensive country. They did not even have the money to buy food. Fortunately, they met a drummer from another band who worked part-time at a local supermarket and who stole food for them.

Although touring was good for the band, its privations were not universally enjoyed by its members.

"On the road it was horrible," recalled Couzens. "We were so broke we became like animals. We fought over food. We fought over money and we took it all out on Howard—he became the band punch-bag."

Andy Couzens recalled how tormenting Howard Jones became light relief for the band.

"One place where we stayed we took all the slats out of his bed," he said, "and it collapsed when he went to bed in it. I guess it's funny the first night, but we did it every night."

Sometimes "The Rhino" (Jones) suffered worse maltreatment. On one occasion, as Couzens recalled: "It was 20 degrees outside, there was a row as usual over someone sitting on a bench in the van, I opened the door and kicked him [Jones] out and left him in the middle of nowhere. He had to walk for an hour and a half before he got back to where we were staying."

They performed twice in Stockholm, on April 23 and 25, and then their last Swedish gig was on April 30 in Lidingö, a satellite town just north-east of Stockholm. One of these shows began in a riot. The police came and the entire audience was arrested.

"Yeah, a mad night," said Couzens, "but all gigs were—the night in Sweden when Ian sucked the barrel of a gun some nutter had pulled, or the night police showed and arrested the whole audience before we went on."

On the whole, though, they were well received.

According to Couzens: "It's not difficult to make it big in Stockholm, it's only a small music scene, especially if you're going out every night, causing the mayhem we did. We were all over the papers and women were chasing after us."

In early May, The Stone Roses returned to England. Now they faced their toughest challenge. They were to play their first gig in Manchester. It would be at the International One, with its capacity for 800 people. Gareth Evans, the owner and future manager of The Stone Roses, made sure that it was full by handing out free tickets around Manchester.

Those people who were there that night said the band were awesome. Their stage act was beginning to evolve into The Stone Roses shows that thousands of fans would later flock to see. The performance began with an intro tape of Tom Jones singing "It's Not Unusual"—one of the first records Ian Brown's auntie had given him when he was seven. Their playing was confident and the tunes expertly executed. And Brown's well-honed aggressive stage persona was finally unleashed on the home crowd. Brown taunted the crowd all night long and they loved it.

"Hey, why don't you over there come here—you might learn something," he would say. Or "Stop talking, fuckers, this is your last chance to dance—anyone who is anyone already knows it." And he ended the show by saying, "Thanks to everyone who came, a pitiful display."

After the International gig, The Stone Roses became a regular touring band. On May 24, they played the

Manchester Gallery under the name The Stone Bozos. The gig was supposed to be recorded by Piccadilly Radio, who wanted to limit the audience to a small circle of dedicated fans. However, the club put out flyers and the radio station then pulled out. The rumor circulated that the band were going to pull out too.

"But we couldn't in the end because everyone knew we were doing it," said Garner. "So we did it anyway. All those people who came to see us knew each other. Word got out fast amongst friends of mine and Reni's and John's and the hardcore mob, the scooter lot. Ian knew them all. You get to know 50 guys pretty well if you're into shit like that."

Now they had got over their prejudice about playing Manchester, they felt they could play anywhere. Like most up-and-coming British bands, they toured the country playing clubs, theaters, and universities.

Next they played another gig in London on July 4, 1985 with Doctor & The Medics, who were a British psychedelic pop-rock band, formed and fronted by Clive Jackson, (a.k.a. The Doctor), in the 1980s. They began a psychedelic revival in 1986 with their UK number one single "Spirit In The Sky," which was a cover of the song by Norman Greenbaum, a former folk singer who had developed his own psychedelic pop in the US during the early 1970s. Doctor & The Medics were known for their wacky make-up and outrageous stage shows but, after "Spirit In The Sky", the band's follow-up releases found no commercial success. Even so, Doctor & The Medics continue touring around Britain to this day and have a loyal cult following.

However, on the same bill, The Stone Roses and Doctor & The Medics made a weird combination.

"I remembered the girls in Doctor & The Medics putting their wigs on in the dressing room and thinking it was pretty funny," recalled Garner. "It looks like a weird gig now, but it was a gig. At the time we would play anywhere—but not in a pub."

The Stones Roses would play any venue that would have them. However, they were ambitious to do something unique that would set them apart from the rest of the local bands. Because of their loyal personal following, the supposedly "secret" gig at the Gallery had actually been something of a success. Steve Adge then came up with an idea that would capitalize on it.

The Stone Roses were still rehearsing at Spirit Studios whenever they got the chance and, one afternoon, Adge approached them.

"He'd been to London, buzzing about a warehouse he'd been to," said Garner.

In London, a new fashion had started for warehouse raves. Disused warehouses were turned temporarily into illegal clubs. All-night or all-weekend raves would be held there. Tickets would be sold, but ticket holders would only be informed of the location of the rave at the last moment, so that the authorities could not close them down. Later they would develop into huge raves held in massive marquees in the countryside outside the city.

Steve Adge wanted to put on a warehouse rave in Manchester. In London, raves employed DJs and rarely had live bands. But Adge thought that The Stone Roses, with the local following, might give his rave more of a Manchester feel. This was exactly the type of thing The Stone Roses had been yearning to do and they jumped at the chance of doing something new and exciting.

With The Stones Roses on board, Steve Adge began organizing his first rave. He telephoned British Railways, who owned warehouses on Fairfield Street behind Manchester's main Piccadilly railroad terminal, and hired one. It was actually underneath one of the railway arches. Once Adge had secured the warehouse and hired The Stone Roses, he printed up tickets. People bought these without knowing how to find their way to the warehouse. However, hand-drawn maps, which showed the route to the rave, were photocopied and distributed. But no starting point was identified. To find that out, the ticket holder had to telephone Spirit Studios. This gave the organizers a double protection against the police finding out.

"If they found out about the gig they'd pull it," said Garner. "And 'The only dress restriction is no blue uniforms!' was handwritten on the tickets."

The first of Manchester's warehouse raves was planned for July 20, 1985. That afternoon, The Stone Roses went down to the warehouse on Fairfield Street. They set up their equipment and did a quick sound check, then went around to Ian Brown's flat to wait until they were needed on stage. While they were waiting, the band chilled with a few of their friends. One of them was Steve Cressa, who would later become, essentially, the fifth member of The Stone Roses as their effects man.

Couzens recalled how Cressa had met up with the band some time earlier: "We met him down in the Berlin club. He was always like a young kid in there, running around being pretty sharp. I spoke to him and he sort of joined the gang. He was one of the few people that we let into the rehearsals and hang around. There were always loads of people that wanted to come down and watch us rehearse but we couldn't really allow it. It would have been really horrible. He was a real culture vulture, always taking in things from other people. Ian looked on Cressa as some sort of entertainments manager."

The Stone Roses and their entourage hung around at Brown's until about 11 o'clock, then made their way back down to Fairfield Street. As the idea of warehouse raves was so new to Manchester, even then, they were not sure if anyone would actually turn up.

When they went into the warehouse, there were hundreds of people milling about and it took the band a moment or two before they realized that these people were their audience. There were so many people packed into place that the band could not even get onto the stage until well after midnight. But when they did, they set the place alight. Each member of the band was on top form that night and the crowd went berserk. Reni, particularly, excelled himself because, for once, he had taken amphetamines like the rest of the band.

"Reni never took speed normally but that night he was really buzzing," recalled Couzens. "Normally he's fast enough as it is but at this gig he was like a hyper version of Keith Moon."

The Stone Roses' performance that night has gone down in music legend and established the band as Manchester's premier live act. The warehouse party was such a success that they put on another one, five months later.

"They were the best two gigs that I ever played with them," Couzens said. "There were nearly 400 people at the second one. It really felt like a major event. It was brilliant."

Playing these warehouse raves gave The Stone Roses a unique understanding of their audience. The people who came to the warehouse gigs had gone to a lot of trouble and effort to see The Stone Roses. This gave the band an empathy with their fans that they would use when writing *The Stone Roses* album.

After the first warehouse rave, they went back into the studio with Martin Hannett and set about working on an album, which they began recording in August. This would have been their debut album and may well have been called *The Stone Roses*. But it was not released at the time. It was only issued a decade later as *Garage Flower*. For this album, they recorded all the songs they had written up to this point. Essentially, they were doing their live set in a studio. It was not a happy experience.

The creative conflicts they had encountered with Martin Hannett when recording their first single were even more pronounced this time around. Recording two tracks with Hannett was difficult enough, but recording 13 was next to impossible. After a great deal of heartache and strife, they finally managed to lay down all the tracks that would go on the album. They were "Getting Plenty," "Here It Comes," "Trust A Fox," "Tragic Roundabout," "All I Want," "Heart On The Staves," "I Wanna Be Adored," "This Is The One," "Fall," "So Young," "Tell Me," "Just A Little Bit," and "Mission Impossible."

As the album was not issued, these recording sessions served only as a educational project. However, it did give them a chance to develop their music further. In many ways, this early album would be a turning point for their music.

The songs that appeared on both *Garage Flower* and *The Stone Roses*—"I Wanna Be Adored" and "This Is The One"—were given a chance to develop into the classic anthems that would define the sound of The Stone Roses.

Because of the problems with Martin Hannett, The Stone Roses never liked this album and did not really want to see it released. Howard Jones concurred and the album was left to gather dust for the next ten years.

"It's probably a good job that it didn't come out at the time," said Couzens, "because like most bands in the studio for the first time, we weren't quite sure what we were doing. We were all really fucked up. The sessions would go on all night. It was a difficult record to record, but I think it was worth bringing it out years later as a document of what we were like in the early days."

However, Couzens recalled how the band developed their songwriting ability during their three-week stint in the studio. "But despite the mayhem, Martin taught us one thing: he taught us how to write."

Together in the studio day after day, they started to listen to a broader spectrum of music—music that was outside of punk and their personal tastes. Squire's interest in The Jesus And Mary Chain provided the vital springboard into influences that would take them back through the pop of the 1960s.

"The Jesus And Mary Chain were a really important band in many respects," said Couzens. "They opened a lot of doors for people like us. Before them you weren't really allowed to listen to loads of groups." Before The Jesus And Mary Chain, punk had practically ostracized certain groups from the canon. "But they turned people on to a lot of great bands.

From that point we started listening to the Stones, the Beatles, the Byrds, the Misunderstood, and 1960s garage bands. The flavor of our songwriting started to change."

Until then, few of The Stone Roses had listened seriously to anything pre-punk. But now they felt they had license to go ahead and listen to earlier music from an earlier era.

Brown opened his ears to these new influences and expressed regret when he said: "I wish I had heard Jimi Hendrix earlier. I wish I had heard his records when I was 12."

So The Stone Roses were moving even farther away from punk rock, incorporating these new influences, and truly becoming The Stone Roses of *The Stone Roses* album.

On August 2, 1985, The Stone Roses went down to London to play the Marquee club again. Then on August 27 they played a gig at the Hacienda. These were opportunities for them to show off what they had learnt in the studio. John Squire was no longer a three-chord punk guitarist. His playing was now tapping directly into 1960s classics. And working with Hannett, however galling, had once again paid dividends.

"Martin Hannett did amazing things to the sound of John's guitar. It was brilliant," said Garner. "Everyone was gob-smacked."

Squire was now using the wah-wah pedal and other effects in his guitar work, while Brown was still breaking all rules when it came to singer-audience interactions.

Speaking about the Hacienda gig, Garner said: "During the encore Ian jumped into the crowd, everyone went mad. We thought he was gone for. We thought that he was going to get killed."

Finally conquering the Hacienda, The Stone Roses had truly made a name for themselves in Manchester and Howard Jones was persuaded to release their single. "So Young" backed with "Tell Me" came out as a double A side on September 9, 1985, six months after they had recorded it. It was only ever released as a 12-inch disc. However, The Stone Roses' musical style had been evolving so fast that, by then, the songs on the single reflected nothing of their current style. "So Young" and "Tell Me" were rudimentary thrash punk rock tracks and showed little of the underlying sophistication that would set The Stone Roses apart from their contemporaries.

Interviewed soon after the single came out Brown was rueful, saying: "Too much enthusiasm and not enough thought went into that record."

He was particularly critical of the lack of any real content in this first single: "They weren't really songs, just a sound. We've learnt how to write now. But because it [the track] was so well-known in Manchester, it's become an albatross and we've got to shake it off. I wouldn't give 20 pence for that single. It's dreadful angst-ridden rock."

Nonetheless, the single did well in Manchester where the band now had an enthusiastic fan base. Beforehand the band's demo had circulated widely among music fans in the city. Recordings of the Piccadilly radio session had also been well received locally. So there had been a ready market for a single. Paula Greenwood, journalist for *Muze*—a music magazine circulating in the Manchester and Liverpool area in the mid-1980s—gave the single a good review, a first for The Stone Roses. And she was impressed with their approach to live performance.

"Every gig is an event," she wrote. "And this, the long awaited debut single, is big, loud and beautiful. They have certainly matured since their demo, and with the help of Martin Hannett they have become smooth and hard."

While their live performances created a local market for the single, in turn, the record attracted more people to their live performances. But outside Manchester the single did not sell well and it did not bring them the national recognition they craved.

They seized the opportunity to go down to London again to play a few gigs over the next month or so. The first was on September 11. They were to play at a book launch for *Destroy: The Sex Pistols 1977* by Dennis Morris, a photographic biography of the Sex Pistols, at the Embassy Club. A famous nightclub since the 1930s, the Embassy was a truly prestigious venue and their first opportunity to rub shoulders with the capital's rock glitterati.

The Stone Roses were to support The Chiefs Of Relief. Formed in 1985, this band had Paul Cook from the Sex Pistols on drums and its lead guitarist and vocalist was Matthew Ashman—the former front man of Malcolm McLaren's other punk creation Bow Wow Wow. With Duncan Greig on keyboards and Lance Burman on bass, The Chiefs Of Relief were pioneering a new form of music around the London club circuit, which later took off in the rest of the UK. The band fused rap, rock, and funk into their own original sound. Their debut single "Freedom To Rock" became a massive dance hit in the UK, and the sound directly inspired the "white rap" sound of The Beastie Boys.

The Stone Roses had been eager to get an opportunity to meet Paul Cook but, in the event, they were sorely disappointed.

"He was like a dull brickie [bricklayer]," remembered Garner. "He had no aura at all."

Afterwards they headed back to Exeter for a second time, where they played the university. They had another gig in London on October 26, at the Riverside Studios arts centre in Hammersmith. Since the 1950s, the Riverside Studios had been home to classic UK music TV shows, including *The Six-Five Special*, *Drum Beat*, *The Old Grey Whistle Test*, and even, for a while, Britain's premier pop showcase *Top Of The Pops*. The first five series of the cult British sci-fi TV classic, *Dr Who*, were filmed there. Then The Stone Roses returned north to play Manchester University on November 22. It was a triumphal homecoming.

As Garner recalled: "It was the first gig where we got out of the van and people carried our gear in for us—there were loads of students helping us to carry our stuff in. Slim was roadying for us with Gluepot Glen. It was an easy day for them."

The Stone Roses played their next gig on November 28 in King George's Hall in Blackburn, a town 20 miles north of Manchester. As their northern fan base continued to grow, Steve Adge organized the second of his warehouse parties, which was held on November 30. This was planned to be an even bigger event than the rave in Fairfield Street, though that had its down side.

"It was a different place," said Garner. "We hired a massive space. It was not as intimate as the first one. There was a dead high ceiling—fucking freezing. I remember doing the sound-check with gloves on."

This time they were holding a warehouse rave in an unheated space in a northern city in the middle of winter. Brown did not even turn up for the technical rehearsal.

"We played these songs all day every day and it wasn't a big deal that Ian didn't go to the sound-check," Garner added. "Andy sang in the sound-check. I've got that on video. It's funny."

They had to film something because the excuse they had used to hire the warehouse from British Rail this time was that they were shooting a pop video.

In the event 1,000 people turned up and the warehouse was warmed by body heat.

Despite their growing following, The Stone Roses felt that their career was not moving ahead as quickly as it ought to be. They were not happy with the album they had recorded with Martin Hannett, and beginning to have their doubts about Howard Jones. So The Stone Roses took their publicity into their own hands. Brown and Reni walked around the city one evening with cans of red spray-paint, daubing "The Stone Roses" on walls and store fronts throughout the town.

Brown explained: "Me and Reni decided we'd been ignored for long enough. We thought we'll cover the city with 'Stone Roses.' So we sprayed everywhere at about seven or eight o'clock at night."

Doing this, they risked arrest.

"Reni was spraying the front of a library," continued Brown, "and there was a copper stood just around the corner—but the copper couldn't see him."

At the time, they denied responsibility, claiming that the spray-paint campaign was the work of a misguided fan.

"People just had this preconceived idea that we were hooligans all the time," Brown had said, "so we were blamed for the graffiti thing. I don't know why everyone got so upset. It was just some mates. We didn't know about it until afterwards. We know who did it but we're not gonna tell."

However, critics pointed out that the graffiti trail traced a bus route from the central library back to their apartment.

The spray-paint publicity campaign was not an original idea.

"We used to go and watch Seventeen," said Couzens. "They were a great power pop mod band who eventually became The Alarm—and wherever they went they sprayed their name."

A punk band formed in the 1978 in Rhyl, Wales, the band took their original name from the Sex Pistols' song "Seventeen," then changed their name in 1981 to The Alarm, after their own track "Alarm, Alarm." They toured the US with U2 and, later, Bob Dylan, and entered the *Billboard* Hot 100 with "Spirit of '76" and "Sold Me Down The River."

The Stone Roses' graffiti brought the band to people's attention, but it damaged their standing in Manchester music circles.

"When Ian and Reni did the graffiti, we thought that this was a really cool idea," said Couzens. "But it finished us off in Manchester. We could get no gigs, no press."

This was largely because they had acquired an enemy in the shape of Tony Wilson, who had taken over running the Hacienda after Howard Jones left. A leading figure in the Manchester music scene, he is the subject of the cult movie *24-Hour Party People*. The movie title was taken from *Squirrel*

And G-Man Twenty Four Hour Party People Plastic Face Carnt [sic] *Smile*—a.k.a. *White Out*—the name of the first album by The Happy Mondays, whose career was inextricably linked to that of The Stone Roses, both as rivals on the Manchester scene and as friends.

The Happy Mondays came from Little Hulton, a northwest suburb on the perimeter of the metropolitan area of Manchester. The members of the band were local drug dealers who decided that they wanted to be rock stars. In the early 1980s, The Happy Mondays formed around brothers, Shaun and Paul Ryder, who provided vocals and bass respectively. From among their drug dealing acquaintances, they gathered guitarist, Mark "Moose" Day, keyboard player, Paul "P.D." Davis, and drummer, Gary "Gaz" Whelan, into the band and they began performing Joy Division covers in local youth clubs.

By 1984, The Happy Mondays had started to work on their own material, inspired by the Detroit acid house that was being played in the Hacienda. They would spend a lot of time partying in the Hacienda, and became the club's regular drug dealers, selling ecstasy tablets to the clientele. It did not take long before they began performing at the club. Once they had regular gigs at the Hacienda, the Ryder brothers recruited their next-door neighbor, Mark Berry (a.k.a. Bez), to the band. Although Bez could not sing or play an instrument, his on-stage dancing became legendary and he remains one of the Madchester's most enduring images.

The Happy Mondays' big break came when they won a "battle of the bands" competition held at the Hacienda. Tony Wilson, who had organized the event, became their manager and signed them to the Factory label. Naturally, it was in Wilson's interest to build up The Happy Mondays by putting down The Stones Roses—the enemies of Factory and the Hacienda—and the graffiti campaign gave him the perfect opportunity to do that.

"Tony Wilson was slagging us off and made moves to make sure that we couldn't do anything," said Couzens. "We tried for a rehearsal room at the Boardwalk and they wouldn't let us in there either."

On the other hand, this gave new credibility to their outlaw status.

As Couzens noted: "We were outsiders. We had total notoriety."

shoot you down

At the beginning of 1986, the local outlook was dire. The Stone Roses were *personae non gratae* and could not get a gig in Manchester. However, they still had a large local fan base and—due in part to the graffiti campaign—everyone knew who they were. The situation called for radical action. They had shelved an album. Now they were going to part company with Howard Jones. They were changing as a group and flinging off the shackles of the past.

"We wanted to move as far away from 'So Young' as possible," said Brown.

They went back to rehearsal, worked tirelessly, and came up with "Sally Cinnamon." This was the first product of a new working method. Previously, the guitarists, Squire and Couzens, would come up with riffs and Brown would then concoct lyrics to accompany them. Now Brown and Squire worked closely together, becoming the core of the band's new songwriting team. As a result Couzens' input became marginalized.

"'Sally Cinnamon' was a sort of semi-conscious effort to shake off 'So Young,' which unfortunately sounded quite Gothy," said Brown. "It was big in The Ritz [a Manchester Goth club]. People actually thought that we were Goths and were pissed off that we had short hair."

At night in Squire's flat, Brown and Squire would construct the melodies and lyrics simultaneously. This way they were able to build up more complex song structures. They would increase the band's modulation, consciously designing louder and quieter passages. There would be softer guitar parts and louder drum segments, deliberately creating a space for each band member. These complex song structures showed adept use of musical technique with false endings and stop-starts, drop downs and long build-ups, well-crafted guitar solos and explosive choruses—all backed by Reni's powerhouse drumming. But their music was not overburdened with the use of these devices. Instead they served to create a more open, soaring soundscape. It was this Brown–Squire writing team that would compose the tracks on *The Stone Roses* album.

Unable to get a gig in Manchester at the beginning of 1986, they managed to secure a booking on March 5 in Blackburn, back at King George's Hall. There they played new Brown and Squire songs, including "Sally Cinnamon," for the first time on stage. These new songs received a less-than-enthusiastic reception.

Next The Stone Roses played Manchester University again, on March 10. Then on March 25, they played Warwick University—its campus is on the outskirts of the historic town of Coventry, 90 miles south of Manchester, between Birmingham and London. On this occasion they supported Love And Rockets, which was formed by some of the ex-members of Bauhaus, who had also performed as Tones On Tail.

"I was a big Bauhaus fan," said Garner, "but in person they were assholes. They would not talk to any of us and didn't want to associate with us. That was their third band in the spotlight. We must have been like little kids to them."

Formed in 1978, Bauhaus were the prototype Goth band. They toured the US in 1980, and later performed the track

"Bela Lugosi's Dead" on screen in the 1983 movie, *The Hunger*, starring David Bowie and Catherine Deneuve. But their initial success was short-lived. They broke up and reformed in various guises. In 1998, after reforming as Bauhaus, they staged two sell-out shows at Hollywood Palladium in Los Angeles.

The attitude of the veterans in Love And Rockets made The Stone Roses feel as if their career had stalled. They now realized that without representation—a manager and a press agent—The Stone Roses could go no further. They probably regretted getting rid of Howard Jones. Then fate intervened. They saw an advertisement in the local paper, which presented them with a golden opportunity.

"We saw an ad saying that they were looking for demos of new bands," said Couzens. "The address was for the International."

It seemed that the International's owner, Gareth Evans, also wanted to get into management.

"So we drove down there and burst into his office, demanding a meeting,"continued Couzens. Jones was cut out of the deal completely. "We never thought that Howard was up to the job. We argued with his ideas. We never signed a contract with him. He never got his dollars out of it."

Pete Garner recalled the meeting with Gareth Evans: "We launched into a massive spiel at him. We were dead cocky. 'You will be our manager,' we told him."

Evans was not cowed by their brashness. He was even more confident than they were that he could make things work for The Stone Roses.

"He told us that he could sell anything to anybody," noted Garner. "He was just halfway through this spiel when he dropped his pants and showed us his underwear. He told us that he was selling those as well—he tried to sell us a pair of pants [undershorts]. It was at that moment that we knew he was the right man for the job."

Gareth Evans had made the International One and Two the coolest rock venues in Manchester, while the Hacienda was beginning to concentrate on dance music. Evans was well known in Manchester for his flamboyant character. More importantly for The Stone Roses, he was totally outside Factory's control. He was his own man.

So the band severed any remaining connections with Howard Jones and retained the services of Gareth Evans. Obviously, Jones wasn't pleased about being dropped as he never really got any financial return from the band.

They signed a contract a week later in a local Spaghetti House restaurant. The contract was witnessed by *Muze* journalist Paula Greenwood, who was still The Stone Roses' major champion in the music press.

As the band's new manager, Gareth Evans let them use International One as their rehearsal room. They could now practice on a fully equipped stage in a large auditorium. This allowed them to develop their sound further. As a band, they were as determined and businesslike as ever.

"We would rehearse every day," said Garner. "Well, you would, wouldn't you? It's your job."

Up in his office, Evans was busy selling the band. He would spend hours on end phoning around local press, music magazines, and record labels. Evans would send out hundreds of tapes. Everyone he phoned got at least one. His major thrust was to push the band into national media consciousness.

With the band working in the International, Evans could use his input to influence their development. Although Brown and Squire's songs had not gone down well in Blackburn, Evans recognized that this new writing partnership was the way forward for the band. He encouraged this and, as it came into its own, they began to write the songs that appear on *The Stone Roses*.

Andy Couzens always believed that changing rehearsal rooms sparked a new bout of creativity. But this time he found himself squeezed out. He blamed Evans.

"Me and Gareth never got on," said Couzens. "We had screaming rows. He would go on at me about loads of things. It was starting to get a bit frustrating."

This frustration would only increase as Brown and Squire started to produce more and more better songs. And they would be written more quickly than at any time before.

Brown and Squire's increased productivity created more problems. The songwriting pair decided that they should get the largest share of the royalties, when the band started to become successful. This, they assumed arrogantly, would be only a matter of time given the new material they had written. One morning they arrived for rehearsals and they told the other members of the band that they would be taking all the songwriting credits from now on. Andy Couzens and Reni stormed out of the rehearsal, almost as soon as they finished speaking and temporarily left the band.

Couzens pointed out: "The argument at that point was about songwriting royalties."

But there was more to it than just the money.

"At first it was more the aesthetic thing of having two names on the labels like 'Lennon/McCartney' etc.," said Couzens. "It looked good. The reason I left the band had nothing to do with money."

Reni rejoined the band quickly. Couzens took longer to return. In the meantime, he had even got himself a regular job.

With everyone back in place and peace restored—for now—The Stones Roses were then booked for a gig in Dublin, Ireland. It was to be Couzens' last performance and the last time that The Stone Roses would play as a quintet.

Evans had booked The Stone Roses to play McGonagles, in Dublin on June 5. It was the first gig Evans had got for them outside of the International where they had been able to sit in as a house band. McGonagles is an important venue, where a lot of foreign bands have made their debut. Evans had put a lot of effort into getting The Stone Roses on the bill there. But unfortunately the man who "could sell anything to anybody" had got them booked in on a heavy metal night.

The Stone Roses' style of music, look, and stage-presentation did not go down well with the audience, who began to heckle. Squire tried to placate the irate crowd by playing Deep Purple's heavy metal classic "Smoke On The Water." But this only served to rile the audience further. For them, seeing some paisley-shirted pansy playing the heaviest of heavy metal riffs verged on sacrilege. Violence erupted and the band retreated back-stage. But when the promoter threaten not to pay them, they simply threatened to join in the altercation.

"You either pay us or we go back out there and the place gets trashed," they said.

The Stone Roses had caused another riot—the third in three years, in three difference countries.

For Couzens it would be his violent farewell to the band. This was ironic as he had started The Stone Roses to get away from violence. While the rest of the band got into the van and took the ferry, Couzens caught an airplane home.

"The gig was booked at short notice and I had arranged to see my girlfriend and had to go to work the next day, so I was in a rush to get back," said Couzens.

Unbeknown to Couzens he was flying straight out of The Stones Roses. And Gareth Evans, seeing this as the final straw, would make sure he never came back.

Losing Couzens was a big blow to the band psychologically. He had, after all, been in the band in all its various forms for seven years. But it did not hurt them musically. Squire was now an accomplished guitarist. He now pushed himself further to fill the musical gap that Couzens had left. Like guitar heroes, Pete Townshend and Jimi Hendrix, he played both lead and rhythm guitar simultaneously. It is now widely accepted that, on *The Stone Roses* album, John Squire showed himself to be one of the greatest guitar players of his generation.

Now a four-piece, The Stone Roses played a handful of gigs over the summer months of 1986 in Manchester, Liverpool, Leeds, and London. At Liverpool's Mardi Gras club, The Stone Roses played "(Song For My) Sugar Spun Sister" for the first time. Other new songs written under the aegis of Evans that would appear on *The Stone Roses* album began to push older songs out of the set. As these were phased out, their music's rockier edge slowly gave way to softer, psychedelic pop.

Pete Garner recalled how the band's onstage material began to change: "We hated doing 'So Young'—it was like our 'White Riot' [The Clash's first single that was requested endlessly], we were really sick of it. John had just bought his first wah-wah pedal and just written 'Elephant Stone.' It was a move forward."

"Elephant Stone" appeared on the American version of *The Stone Roses*, though not on the version released in the UK. With it any pretense at punk was lost. It was a dance tune with a funk feel.

Squire would became a great exponent of the wah-wah pedal, which had fallen out of fashion after Hendrix died in 1970. Punk and its progeny preferred crisp, sharp riffs. Now John created a new sound on his guitar, which tapped right back into the sound of the 1960s.

On December 12, Evans arranged for The Stone Roses to record their first demo as a four-piece band. They recorded four new songs, "Elephant Stone," "Going Down," "Sugar Spun Sister," and "Sun Still Shines." While making this demo, The Stone Roses began taking an active interest in their own production. Pete Garner even produced the mono mixes of "Sun Still Shines" himself. Again Evans made sure that everybody in the music business got a copy.

On January 30, they played their first major gig back in Manchester, headlining in the International One. At this performance they found they had attracted a new audience. Their old post-punk following had disbanded, but new, younger music fans were starting to take an interest. This was probably due to the demos that Evans had sent out. Over a year had passed since they had sprayed the city with graffiti and, at last, The Stone Roses were beginning to live down their image as ruffians. Now their music was central. Leery punk posturing had given way to perfect guitar-based pop.

Evans was still ringing everyone and anyone to raise some interest in the band. After almost a solid month spent on the phone Evans got interest from a small label in Wolverhampton named FM Revolver. It was run by Paul Birch, the man who The Stone Roses would daub with paint three years later. Birch had a partner called Dave Roberts, who freelanced for *Sounds* magazine.

With a FM Revolver recording contract in his sights, Evans decided to build up The Stones Roses' fan-base to help pressure the label into cutting a deal. To do this Evans had The Stone Roses headline at the International One, again, and pull his old trick of giving away free tickets to draw in a capacity crowd. After he had covered the Stone Roses gig there in a very favourable review in Sounds, Dave Robert—wearing his hat as a partner in FM Revolver—persuaded his colleague Paul Birch to take the band on. Once they were signed to the label, Roberts saw to it that The Stone Roses were pushed to the top of the company's release schedule.

The ploy worked. A few days later The Stone Roses took a trip down the motorway to Wolverhampton, with Evans, to sign a contract with Paul Birch. This stated that FM Revolver would release only one single on a subsidiary Black Records label, set up for this purpose. It was a new beginning. On the way back to Manchester, Evans, who had a box full of "So Young" singles in his car, threw them out onto the expressway so cars drove over them.

"That's the ghost of Howard Jones removed forever," said Evans. "The new era starts now." Then they sped back to Manchester.

Gareth Evans continued to arrange capacity performances for The Stone Roses at the International. As a result, the band decided they would no longer play support acts elsewhere. Evans no doubt shared this view. He was convinced that if they acted like a big band they would ultimately become one. They were fast becoming the biggest act in Manchester. However, they were still more-or-less unknown nationally, but they hoped that their new single "Sally Cinnamon" would alter that.

"Sally Cinnamon" was released on May 28, 1987, backed with the tracks, "Here It Comes" and "All Across The Sands." With it, The Stone Roses had said a final goodbye to any remnant of their punk sound. "Sally Cinnamon" was a melodic pop tune, accurately demonstrating the band's new direction. They put out 1,000 copies and sold them all. It cemented their reputation in Manchester, but still did not make any impact in the rest of the UK.

That summer they played a series of gigs around northern England. But beforehand, Pete Garner announced that when they got back he would like to leave the band. They played the International One once more on June 26. It now seemed like home. Then they played Take Two in Sheffield in the neighboring county of Yorkshire in July. Afterward they played two gigs in Liverpool—one in a small club called Planet X; the other before a larger audience at the Larks In The Park festival on August 11. This was their first open-air performance, and the last time Garner would play with them.

When Garner left The Stone Roses there was no animosity between him and the remaining members. He even offered to play with them until they found someone to replace him. His reasons for leaving are open to speculation. It could have been that The Stone Roses' changing style had left him behind musically, or perhaps he felt that the band without Couzens no longer appealed to him. As it was, they would not have to look too far for a replacement.

Over the summer, despite the uncertainty concerning the band's line-up, their set had come together and a lot of the tracks that would appear on the The Stone Roses album were now part of their regular repertoire. Now to finalize their line-up, they needed a new bass player, someone who fitted into the band. They began auditioning fruitlessly, when the choice should have been obvious. They should have called Mani.

Mani had not been wasting his time since The Waterfront had broken up. When he was not watching his beloved Manchester United Football Club playing soccer, he sat in his room practicing the bass and gigging with local garage bands. He was now proficient, but the call never came. He only heard that The Stone Roses needed a bass player by accident, through the grapevine.

"I knew Ian and John already," said Mani. "We were ex-punks kicking about on the Manchester scooter scene, digging Motown and Northern Soul. I'd been in a band with John—The Waterfront, with Andy Couzens and Chris Goodwin—so he knew I was capable. I found out that the Roses needed a new bass player through my brother Greg. I got hold of Squire's number and called him up. 'The job's mine,' I said. Simple as that. They were sick of auditioning bassists and John sounded relieved. 'We should have come to you first,' he said."

Couzens particularly was glad that Mani was back in the band.

"Mani was just the same then as he is now, exactly the same guy," he said. "The one thing about being in a band is that you never have to grow up. If you make enough money you never have to do anything. You can be 17 or 18 for the rest of your life."

Mani brought a special cohesion to the band. When he began to play with The Stone Roses at the International Two on November 13, the band seemed to come together in a way it had never done before. They were now the classic quartet that would produce a classic album.

Towards the end of 1987 the band just rehearsed as much as they could to meld Mani into the new line-up. They had started to get good reviews in the national music press on the strength of their shows at the International. It seemed they were just about to break into the big time.

At the beginning of 1988, the band decided to record their third single, the dance track "Elephant Stone." A London-based label, named Rough Trade, paid for the recording, although The Stone Roses were not actually signed to the label. While this took place, Gareth Evans was working on long-term deals with other parties.

"At the time we nearly signed to Rough Trade," said Brown. "In fact, Rough Trade signed us to do 'Elephant Stone' with Peter Hook."

Hook was the bassist from New Order.

"When 'Elephant Stone' was ready to record, we started to look for someone good to produce a dance record, and we hit on his name," said Brown.

Again The Stone Roses found themselves sleeping with the enemy. But now that The Stone Roses had moved into dance music, they had changed their attitude to Factory.

"We had rated New Order's dance tunes, and Peter Hook just liked our song, I think," commented Brown.

Evans arranged for The Roses to work with New Order's Peter Hook, who had liked the group's "Sally Cinnamon" single. He oversaw the production of "Elephant Stone," which did a lot to bring The Stone Roses to the attention of a wider audience.

"Elephant Stone" was recorded in Yellow 2 studios in Stockport.

The B-side to the single was "Full Fathom Five." Fooling around in the studio, they came up with the idea of reverse tracking. They ran the tape of "Elephant Stone" backward and put a new drum track over the top. This was the first time that they had used reverse tracks on their recordings and it was a technique they would use on *The Stone Roses* album on the track "Don't Stop."

"It's our third single but we're all looking on it as a debut as it's the first one we all feel really behind," noted Brown.

"Elephant Stone" was the first completed track for *The Stone Roses* album they now intended to record. The single was not released immediately as they were in limbo over an album deal. While Rough Trade were eager to sign them, Gareth Evans was also in negotiations with the UK arm of the huge South African publishing house, Zomba.

The Stone Roses wanted Peter Hook to produce the album, but he had other commitments and Geoff Travis, who owned Rough Trade, suggested that they work with John Leckie.

"As we were doing 'Elephant Stone' Geoff Travis said try John Leckie, I think he'll be good for you," recalled Brown.

John Leckie was a well-respected producer. He had begun in the music business as a tea boy at the famous Abbey Road Studios, bringing beverages to the likes of Pink Floyd and former members of The Beatles. Leckie was quickly promoted to tape operator and began working with those he had previously been plying with drinks. After recording with Pink Floyd and George Harrison, he gained enough experience to produce small acts himself, notably the punk band XTC.

XTC came from Swindon, 70 miles west of London, and were formed in 1977—the year the Sex Pistols came to prominence. However, XTC's music bore little relation to the Sex Pistols' output. They were a throwback to the basics of punk, such as the New York Dolls, and added quirky art-pop rhythms, and odd melodic twists, to the basic punk thrash. They released albums throughout the 1980s, on both sides of the Atlantic, with mediocre chart success, though their music consistently received rave reviews in the music press.

Leckie's first producing job was on XTC's *White Music* album. This made his name. In 1987 XTC released a pastiche psychedelic album under the pseudonym of Dukes Of Stratosphear. This was also produced by Leckie. It attracted a lot of attention and gave them a cult following in both the UK and the US.

The Dukes' *Psonic Psunspot* album showcased Leckie's talent as a producer and made him fashionable to work with.

So The Stone Roses got in contact with him and discussed making an album.

"We met John Leckie and we got on," said Brown. "We thought that the Dukes Of Stratosphear LP had a good range of sounds. A clever mind had made it. And obviously he had a good knowledge of equipment."

Leckie was not overly impressed with The Stone Roses when he first saw them at a live gig.

As he said: "They were a bit of a shambles the first time I saw them."

But he was impressed by Reni's drumming: "I got the impression that Reni was the star of the show and a lot of people had just come to hear him drum."

They were playing the larger International Two in Manchester for the first time. It was a benefit gig for AIDS awareness, and to raise money to campaign against the Conservative government's "Clause 28," which aimed to outlaw the so-called promotion of homosexuality in schools. In the audience were Liam Gallagher and his brother—and one-time Roses' roadie—Noel. Seeing The Stone Roses on stage inspired them to start UK rock giant, Oasis.

Also on the bill were the Manchester folk-rock band, James, whose 1993 album, *Laid*, earned them a cult following on the west coast of the US. They had toured the US with Neil Young, joined Peter Gabriel's WOMAD tour, and played on the *David Letterman Show*, though some of their more sexually suggestive lyrics were censored.

James were supposed to headline. But this was an important showcase gig and, in an attempt to be true to the vow, never to support another act again, The Stone Roses went around town replacing the official posters with their own, which put them top of the bill. They also went on late and prolonged their set, limiting the time James could play. But crucially, it was the first time that they opened their set with "I Wanna Be Adored." From then on they would always open with it and not only in live shows—it also opens *The Stone Roses* album.

Even though Leckie thought The Stones Roses were shambolic on stage, he was impressed by their recording potential.

"What struck me most when I first heard The Stone Roses' demo was immediately how much more commitment they had than most bands you hear," he said.

He made dizzying comparisons: "Try playing The Beatles' *Revolver* or some of Captain Beefheart's albums and The Roses really stand up," said Leckie. "Technically maybe they don't quite match the records made nowadays. But the melodies, the quality of the singing, and the overall construction of the songs are classic. You can't beat a good combination of a good tune, a good rhythm, a good sound, and a good arrangement."

It was now up to Gareth Evans to secure an album deal.

"Zomba were offering us eight LPs," said Brown, "and Rough Trade were only offering an LP or two."

In many ways, signing with Rough Trade was the better option as they were more prominent in the UK market and had bands of a similar caliber on their books. But The Stone Roses wanted to be in the music business for the long haul.

After a great deal of haggling Evans secured a £27,500 ($40,000) advance and they signed with Zomba. Even though they had been introduced to John Leckie by Rough

Trade, he agreed to produce what was now to become their debut album.

Having always considered themselves Manchester outsiders, they chose not to record in Manchester. Instead they would work initially in Battery Studios in Willesden, north-west London, not far from Abbey Road. The record label found them a flat in nearby Kensal Rise, and gave them £10 ($15) a day for food. Living together again, as they had done in Stockholm, reinforced their sense of unity and no doubt helped them during the long recording sessions. They recorded half of the album in Battery Studios, then finished it off in Konk Studios (the Kinks-owned studios) in north east London.

In the studio, John Leckie set himself defined objectives. As he said at the time: "I think that my job as a producer is to make a record that showcases the band, which is certainly true of the way I work with The Stone Roses. I think their record should sound like their best gig. And so I try get them into that sort of mood and that sort of frame of mind when we're recording. It's the same with the mix."

As well as capturing the band's overall sound, Leckie wanted to give space to each individual's contribution.

"I think it's good to highlight everyone's little bit," he said.

Like the band, Leckie was a perfectionist and looking back, he reflected: "As an album *The Stone Roses* was quite difficult to record because we set ourselves a very high standard and scrapped a lot of songs."

Brown agreed: "We wanted to be the best of everything, to be all things to all people at all times. Aim for the stars and you're gonna hit the ceiling. Never put up with second best."

But there was conflict.

"I was specific that they should play as a unit, but they didn't want to sound like they sounded live," said Leckie. "At the same time they wanted to have a band sound, which meant the drums and bass have to be real." He prevailed. "We pushed ourselves hard to make sure that we got good live takes with no session players so that they could reproduce them live."

Leckie shared a sense of humor with the band and he became one of the gang. He liked the democratic approach they had to their music and was impressed by their work ethic.

"There was no discernible musical leader," recalled Leckie. "Each member of the band was equally important. They hardly ever drank. Ian Brown didn't even drink any beer. That impressed me. Plus they had a crazy manager in Gareth Evans, which is always a big help in my book."

Leckie was well used to the madness of the music industry.

"People take more notice of a crazy manager than a sane and sensible one," he pointed out. "If he's crazy and bolshie, he'll get noticed more by the record companies and the press."

Like the band, Evans had total commitment.

"People really do respond to total belief," recalled Leckie. "Gareth forces it upon you endlessly. Even now, after two years, he still phones me up and chews my ear about how great The Stone Roses are. My wife always says there is more to life than The Stone Roses, but you wouldn't believe it the way Gareth talks."

In Battery Studios, The Stone Roses laid down the classic tracks, "I Wanna Be Adored," "Waterfall," and "She Bangs The Drums," recorded in a series of marathon studio sessions. At the same time, Brown and Squire were developing a new song. This was "Made Of Stone," which would become their foremost anthem. This is generally considered to be the best track on the UK version of the album.

According to Squire, the song is "about making a wish and watching it happen—like scoring a goal in a cup final, on a Harley Electroglide, dressed as Spiderman."

Some consider it to be derivative. Writing in *Uncut* magazine, Creation label boss, Alan McGee, argued that The Stone Roses' sound was shaped by The Jesus And Mary Chain, a little-known American band called The Three O'Clock, and Creation's own Primal Scream—for years, critics have argued that The Stone Roses' "Made of Stone" was a rip-off of Primal Scream's "Velocity Girl". According to McGee, other influences included The Byrds, the Adverts, Johnny Thunders, The New York Dolls, George Clinton, and *Planet of the Apes*.

After moving to Konk Studios, the band recorded "This Is The One," "Sugar Spun Sister," "Shoot You Down," and "Bye Bye Badman." This only gave them eight tracks, so Brown and Squire set to work writing again. They came up with "Elizabeth My Dear," a minute-long version of "Scarbrough Fair" with a new lyric about dethroning Queen Elizabeth and killing her. It was a parody of punk, echoing the sentiment of the Sex Pistols' "God Save The Queen" with a nod to Simon and Garfunkel's track "Parsley, Sage, Rosemary, and Thyme," the American duo's 1966 recording of the traditional folk song.

"Maybe Simon and Garfunkel vandalized the original, which is 400 years old—I never got to hear that one," said Brown. "We wanted it to be a familiar tune so that people would instantly identify with it and then hear the lyric clearly."

Another track was created by reversing "Waterfall"—as they had done on "Full Fathom Five," the B-side to the, as yet unreleased, "Elephant Stone" single. Brown claimed that this came about by chance.

"It was accidental," he said. "We got a tape of 'Waterfall' on the port-a-studio, which plays both sides. It sounded great backwards. We could hear lyrics coming out, with strange words suggesting themselves. We went back into the studio, turned the tape over, put the vocal down, and then put a forward drum over it. That's my favorite thing on the first LP. There's 20 seconds at the end that's a killer, when that little rhythm comes in."

This was how "Don't Stop" was born. These reverse songs would become another trademark of The Stone Roses. Unfortunately, the results were often hit and miss, and "Don't Stop" is generally considered the best of them.

Squire also thought "Don't Stop" was one of the best tracks on the album.

"I liked 'Don't Stop' a lot," said Squire. "It's the tape of 'Waterfall' backward, with the bass drum triggered and the only real overdubs are the vocals and a bit of cowbell. I wrote the lyrics by listening to 'Waterfall' backward and writing down what was suggested the vocal might have been. It's good fun doing that, because you sort of remove your involvement from the song. You don't really know what's going to come next."

One of the unique features of *The Stone Roses* is how the tracks are fused together to produce a seemingly organic progression through the album. This did not happen by accident.

"We had beginnings and endings worked out for all the songs," said Brown. "Everything was thought out. 'Sugar Spun Sister,' for example, had to finish on a particular chord. We were absolutely sure how it should be. We were so well prepared. The Stone Roses never winged it. We never had to."

"I Wanna Be Adored" was the obvious song to start the album with as it was the song that the band now used to open their live performances. But although the album was nearing completion, they still needed a song equally strong to close with. *The Stone Roses* was an album that cried out for a huge finale. This would come in the form of an epic 12-minute track, which grew from a tiny squib that they used to play during their sound-checks.

"'I Am The Resurrection' started out as a reverse piss-take of Paul McCartney on 'Taxman,'" recalled Reni. In The Stone Roses' version, the chord sequence is played backwards. "Mani used to play that riff everyday. Then I'd come in and John would doodle some Fender over the top and we'd do it for a laugh at sound-checks. Finally we said, 'Let's do it properly—this joke song actually sounds good.'"

"I Am The Resurrection" would become another classic Stone Roses' anthem. The title and lyric were lifted from a billboard they saw in Manchester.

"The song is to do with church publicity," Reni said. "There was a big church in town that had a big yellow day-glo sign up with that line on it."

The song was criticized for being anti-Christian, but Brown maintained that this was not the case.

"I saw a poster with these words in fluorescent paint on the door of a church and the line impressed me," said Brown. "So this lyric is about anti-Christianity? If people have a normal brain, they should find out how false this accusation is. But sometimes people need mental support even though they understand the real meaning. It's either very sad or very ironic, but the Church is making money, the Roman Catholic Church is the richest religious organization in the world. Everyone must know that."

The Stone Roses went out to Rockfield Studios in Wales to add the final touches to the album. When it was finished, they knew it was something special. But being perfectionists, they were not completely happy with it, seeing only its flaws. They also felt that they had started to move in another musical direction, darker and more dance-orientated than *The Stone Roses* album.

Squire later characterized the album as "twee."

"I think it was mainly the production," he said. "We saw there being a huge gulf between the developing live sound of The Stone Roses and that first album. It was mostly recorded on an SSL desk, and it just didn't sound fat or hard enough."

Along with his gripes with the production, Squire was also aware of his own shortcomings.

"From a guitar point of view I see my approach as the main failing," he said. "I completely deconstructed what I played live and rewrote everything for the studio. That just seems a bit simple, and the switch from chordal to solo stuff just doesn't work. The album just doesn't have the stamp of a real guitar player to me, apart from a couple of solos. It sounds like a two-guitar band, which we weren't."

Ian Brown was more sanguine: "I don't think it matters whether it's a debut album or not, we achieved what we wanted to achieve. We still hadn't recorded the ultimate album, but it was a good start. If we'd had more experience, the first LP would sound more like 'Fool's Gold' than it does, because we still saw all those songs as being dance tracks."

"Fool's Gold" does appear on the American version of the album, but not on the original April 1989 UK release of *The Stone Roses*. "Fool's Gold" noticeably has a more clearly defined dance feel than any of the tracks that appear on the UK original.

"When we played them live, everyone was dancing to them," said Brown. "Not just bobbing up and down, proper dancing."

A perfectionist like Squire, Brown also saw failings in the production, but it did not concern him at the time: "The production of the LP isn't really where we're at, but the songs are strong so they come through. I thought it could be a lot better, and I wish we could have done more with it, but at the end of the day, we decided to let it go. The next album will be even better though. We know a lot more now. We've learnt how to play our instruments better."

With *The Stone Roses* album more or less completed, Zomba released the single, "Elephant Stone," in October 1988, on Silvertone, an offshoot label revived specifically for the band. The sleeve featured Squire's Jackson Pollock-style artwork, which would feature on *The Stone Roses* album and subsequent releases. The single did mediocre business, only just sneaking into the indie chart at first. The Stone Roses were not perturbed; producing an album that they were actually happy with had given the band great confidence.

"Elephant Stone" eventually went to number eight in the UK charts after the success of *The Stone Roses* album in the UK and was subsequently added to the version of the album released in the US.

To promote the single, and pave the way for the UK release of the album, The Stone Roses played out the year with a few small shows. On November 29, they played The Citadel club in St Helens, a large industrial town 20 miles west of Manchester on the eastern outskirts of Liverpool. The Stone Roses then played the Olives club in Chester, a very old town 30 miles south-west of Manchester near the Welsh border. Their live performance now was pretty much what appears on *The Stone Roses* album.

The band then went and played in Scotland for the first time with a gig at The Venue, in the capital city of Edinburgh. They were also scheduled to play at the Rico club in Greenock, a satellite town of Glasgow, Scotland's second city. Unfortunately, Ian Brown had tonsillitis and the Greenock gig was cancelled.

The Stone Roses managed to get their first television appearance in 1988. The show they appeared on was hosted by the Hacienda's Tony Wilson, the manager of The Happy Mondays, who had tried to scupper The Stones Roses' career after their graffiti campaign. It had hardly helped that they had taken Gareth Evans, owner of the International as their manager.

"Wilson did the Hacienda and our manager did the International and they were rivals so Wilson never used to give us any space," said Ian Brown.

However, despite the animosity between their managers, The Stone Roses and The Happy Mondays were good friends. Thanks to the insistence of The Happy Mondays' bassist Paul Ryder, The Stone Roses got television exposure to promote their single and create an audience for the forthcoming release of The Stone Roses album.

"The only reason we got on was because Paul Ryder told Tony Wilson we should be on his show," recalled Brown.

Photographer Ian Tilton, who would go on to photograph The Stone Roses a great deal throughout their career, took pictures of the band during this performance. These pictures would comprise the inner sleeve of The Stone Roses album. They showed the band members in regular jeans and T-shirts. However, when they came to promote the album, they had adopted a completely new style.

In the summer of 1988, ecstasy culture had taken off in Britain's cities. Manchester was at the forefront of this and the Hacienda quickly became a club-Mecca of E. It was playing acid house music to sweaty crowds of ecstasy-fuelled partygoers. This shifted the whole focus of music in Manchester further toward dance music. Before, The Stone Roses had always opposed what was coming out of the Hacienda. Now they adopted the new culture. They abandoned the tight-fitting Mod look and adopted their trademark "baggy" style of dress. They wore loose-fitting jeans and big T-shirts, though Ian Brown took this fashion one step further by wearing flares. When questioned about the band's diverse choice of pants, he replied: "Trousers? Well, them three wear parallels, but I wear flares. But definitely not over 21 inches. It's ridiculous. You look like a clown."

For Brown there was a philosophy behind his new look.

"Why do I wear flares?" he said. "Because they swing when you walk so it's perpetual motion. It's important for your state of mind. It's also important that they come right down to the bottom of the floor so your shoes are obscured, cause if you've got half-mast trousers on then you look like an idiot as well."

Flares were comfortable and he did not mind being ridiculed over them.

"When you walk down the street with a pair of 21-inch hipsters on, it's like being in the house with your slippers on," said Brown. "I get laughed at more than stared at. It doesn't bother me. I'd rather be laughed at than not, every time."

Despite the mockery, Brown and his fellow band members began to be fashion-setters. It was around this time that Reni acquired his famous floppy hat: "It was a brilliant floppy hat that I used to wear in a lot of photos. It had stripes round it and sun signs on it, very old and faded, but really cool. It was a real trend-setting hat."

Although a lot of people began to copy what they did, The Stone Roses—in fashion as well as music—were very much their own men.

As Brown pointed out: "We've never meant to be the slaves of fashion or the clothes, the music or even the attitude, if you always take notice of what other people do, you wouldn't make anything original. I think some independent people would follow fashion in order to discover their own identity somehow."

The Stones Roses' new flamboyant style was a reflection of the confidence they had in the album.

"If I thought we were going to continue selling 2,000 records I'd give in now," said Brown at the time. "But seriously I think we're going to be huge. You can't keep a good band down."

At the beginning of 1989, The Stones Roses' continued their tour of the UK, perfecting the live performance of the songs that appeared on the album. They played gigs at the Legends club in Warrington, before moving on to Sheffield University, 35 miles east of Manchester. Then they played a crucial gig at Middlesex Polytechnic, in Tottenham, northeast London, on February 23.

It was only a small gig in the college commissary, but a journalist from the influential *Melody Maker* magazine, named Bob Stanley, was there. Effectively he was given a live preview of *The Stone Roses* album and wrote the band a rave review.

"They sound like someone has sneaked a tab into your Tizer [a popular British brand of soda]," wrote Stanley. "They sound like the best thing I ever heard."

The Stone Roses brought the tracks of the album to their hometown when they played the Hacienda on February 27. Since they had played there in 1985, the club had changed from a venue for live bands into a DJ-led nightclub. The Stone Roses, though, were not disconcerted. The concert was sold-out and they went on stage with guitars blazing, overwhelming the awestruck audience with their dance-rock fusion.

This gig at the Hacienda was filmed for a late-night TV music program, named *Snub*, on BBC Two. When it was aired, it sparked a media frenzy. In the age of electronic music, The Stone Roses had brought guitar-based music back to prominence. Suddenly they were hot property.

Brown was not fazed by what the press claimed was their overnight success.

"It didn't happen overnight," he insisted. "It took five years. Five years of rehearsals and shitty cassettes, and slightly better demo tapes. We were looking at the Pistols and the Beatles and the Byrds and thinking we could compete with them. We would just try and compete on that level. I couldn't really see any point in aiming low."

The Stone Roses released "Made Of Stone" in March 1989. It was the first track taken from the UK version of the album and would finally give the band their first taste of national success. *Melody Maker's* rival, the *New Music Express* (*NME*), named it their single of the week, and it received extensive airplay on the BBC's music station Radio One. Although "Made Of Stone" is a classic pop track, it reached number four in the indie chart and broke its way into the official top 100 chart, eventually peaking at number 20.

What impressed the media about this track was Brown's skill as a lyricist. He claimed that the lyrics were inspired by a ten-day hitchhike he had taken some time before.

"I've always been on the move," Brown told the press. "When I lived in Sale I never hung about there. I hung about with lads all over the city. I'd been to every seaside resort in England and most of the cities, and I'd been to most of Europe, before we toured. Moving about, it's what I'm into doing."

The single established the band in the eyes of the British public.

"When 'Made Of Stone' was 'single of the week' in the *NME*, that was when we realized that the press knew we existed," said Brown. "We'd already sold out International One and Two and the Hacienda. At the time we could play anywhere in Manchester, but in London we'd maybe get 200 people. After 'Made Of Stone' it went POW! And you couldn't get into our London gigs. It felt right, it felt natural, it felt like we were in the right place at the right time."

As they continued their UK tour, they found that they were hot enough to get a booking in a different part of the country practically every night. They played the Escape Club in Brighton, on the south coast, on February 28, the Club Rio in Bradford 30 miles northeast of Manchester, on March 1, the Venue in the Welsh capital, Cardiff, on March 2, JBs in Dudley near Birmingham, on March 3. These gigs were not particularly well attended, but through word of mouth The Stone Roses' reputation was being built up. *Sounds* magazine and the *NME* gave these preview gigs rave reviews.

"These brightest of sparks actually do merit your attention," said the *NME*.

In April 1989, The Stone Roses finally released their debut album *The Stone Roses*. Although the band was not entirely happy with it, it was an instant success. The music press lauded it with critical acclaim.

"In guitar pop terms, this is a masterpiece," wrote *Sounds* magazine.

Record Mirror called The Stone Roses: "The only young band around at the moment with the potential and balls to go all the way."

Melody Maker (April 29, 1989) hailed John Squire as the new generation's great guitarist: "The spine of the LP is John Squire's guitar playing. Beautifully flowing, certainly psychedelic, there are elements of Hendrix (especially on "Shoot You Down") and Marr (check out the fade to "Bye Bye Badman"), but the rest is the lad's own work."

The only UK music magazine that did not give the album an enthusiastic review straight away was the *NME*. Plainly they repented and they later named it their album of the year. Later still, they would go on to rank it as the number one album of the 1980s.

"A shining embodiment of everything rock music should be," wrote *NME* then. "Arrogant, elegantly crafted and imbued with a rare ability to make its listener feel mighty."

The *NME* thought so highly of *The Stone Roses* that it was ranked number five in their "Greatest Albums Of All Time" list in 1993, while Q magazine ranked *The Stone Roses* fourth in their "Best 100 Albums Of All Time" list in 1998.

"With a swagger not lost on anyone with the ears to hear it," wrote Q, "Manchester's Stone Roses created a debut album that worked on every possible level. Hindsight only confirmed what first listening suggested; that the band had re-defined the landscape of British rock and set a template for the 1990s. Drawing on the ecstatic energy of the late-80s, dance culture and the classic song-based traditions of UK pop, they revitalised the whole scene from both ends of the spectrum simultaneously."

After a decade of electronic dance music, *The Stone Roses* sparked a renaissance of rock 'n' roll in the UK and Britpop was born. The album is a bone fide classic and still sounds fresh and relevant when played today, over 15 years later.

The Stone Roses' sleeve was designed by Squire, with a green background covered with black, white, and gray paint in drips and splashes, as already mentioned, like a painting by Jackson Pollock. Squire painted all of the artwork for The Stone Roses in this style.

"I copied Jackson Pollock because I assumed it would be impossible to get permission to use one of his originals on a record cover," said Squire. "I just copied him and quite enjoyed doing it. And then Reni wanted it doing to his kit. Then we did the guitars as well."

The Clash, one of the band's earliest influences, were also fans of Jackson Pollock. Squire drew further inspiration from the surreal blue and orange colors in the linoleum his parents had laid in the bathroom at home, while the green was "inspired by the water at the Giant's Causeway in [Northern] Ireland, where we went before a gig at Coleraine University." Finally he added broad red, white, and blue stripes and some slices of lemon.

Squire's artwork was entitled, "Bye Bye Badman," and drew its inspiration from the song and the 1968 Paris riots. The lemons on the cover are supposed to represent the lemons that the Paris rioters used to counteract the police's tear gas.

"I bought a lot of lemons," said Squire. "We had a big budget."

He pointed out the lemons are not actually part of the picture.

"They're real lemons, nailed on because it was photographed on the wall—the photographer didn't have a rostrum camera," he said. "It ties in with the lyrics of 'Bye Bye Badman.' It's to do with the Paris student uprisings in May 1968. Me and Ian saw a documentary and liked the clothes: there was a guy, chucking stones, with really nice jacket and desert boots. The students used to suck on lemons to nullify the effects of the tear gas. That's why the *tricolore* is there.

Ian Brown tells a slightly different story which harks back to the trips he made backpacking around the Continent.

"The story behind the lemons on the cover of the first album," said Brown, "is that when we were in Paris we met this 65-year-old man who told us that if you suck a lemon, it cancels out the effects of CS gas. He still thought that the government in France could be overthrown one day—he'd been there in 1968 and everything. So he always carried a lemon with him so that he could help out at the front. At 65, what a brilliant attitude."

Q magazine named the cover of *The Stone Roses* as one of the "100 Greatest Record Covers Of All Time." As one critic pointed out: "No band that sports citrus fruit on its album sleeve is in danger of taking itself too seriously."

i am the resurrection

After the release of *The Stone Roses*, The Stone Roses continued their UK tour. Despite the critical acclaim that the album had brought them, their next gig on the South Parade Pier in Portsmouth on April 28, 1989 was not very well attended. The turnout for the performance at Brunel University in Uxbridge, west of London—where much of Stanley Kubrick's movie classic, *A Clockwork Orange*, was filmed in 1971—the following day was not much better. However, their next gig at Liverpool Polytechnic on May 4 drew a huge crowd. From then on the gigs would get bigger and bigger.

The Queen's Hall in Widnes, a small town just over 20 miles west of Manchester, was packed. It also drew in a bunch of journalists. Although The Stone Roses had only just started to attract media recognition, they already felt they were being hounded and adopted a very arrogant attitude with the press.

"We're not arrogant, we are real," said Squire that night, when a journalist from *Uptown* magazine objected to their surly attitude. "What do you want? A bunch of fakes with prepared answers?"

From then on, when The Stone Roses were not being downright obstreperous, they would conduct interviews in a childish manner, remain silent, respond with monosyllabic answers, or turn the questions back on to their interviewers.

On May 6, The Stone Roses returned to Manchester and played to a sell-out crowd in International Two. Evans no longer needed to hand out free tickets. The show was a huge success. Manchester was well and truly in their hands.

Over the next three months, The Stone Roses played almost 30 dates across the UK. The tour would reach its climax on August 12 at the Empress Ballroom in Blackpool, the foremost resort town on the north-west coast of England. People from Manchester would vacation there, or visit for weekends or day trips, and they could depend on a large contingent of their hometown fans making the trip.

"We wanted to play Blackpool to give people a day out to finish their summer," said Brown. "When you've got no money and you live in Manchester there's nowhere else to go. It's the local seaside resort."

Brown had little time for the resort itself.

"I've been beaten up a few times in Blackpool," he said. "At night if you don't wear a tie you won't get into a pub, and if you're walking the streets people bang into you."

But their fans turned out in droves and the band could not wait to get on stage.

Brown expressed himself back then: "I'm dying to get on, there's a great atmosphere—4,000 people have come here for the day, hung out at the fair and on the beach. They're going to see The Stone Roses and then go and have a party."

The Stone Roses' gig at the Empress Ballroom is considered to be the finest of all their live performances. Finally The Stone Roses had conquered not just Manchester but the entire British Isles.

On July 15, 1989, while the band were still touring the UK, Silvertone released their first post-album single—"She Bangs The Drums" backed with "Standing Here" on a seven-inch disc. Simultaneously, they released the twelve-inch version with two B-sides—"Mersey Paradise" and "Simone." All three B-sides were new songs. This typifies The Stone Roses attitude. Even though they had an acclaimed album in the stores, they were never satisfied and were always striving to move forward with their music. "She Bangs The Drums" entered the UK charts at 36, climbing to 34.

With a strong UK following and modest chart success, The Stone Roses began to widen their horizons. They believed that *The Stone Roses* album showed that they had the potential to become the biggest band in the world. The next step was to return to Europe to showcase the album's tracks. On October 11, they played in Amsterdam, Holland. However, either the band or the audience—probably both—were very stoned and the gig was not particularly well received.

The next day, The Stone Roses played the Les Inrockuptibles Festival in Paris, France. As if to make up for the poor performance the night before, they pulled out all the stops. The fact that half of the crowd was from Manchester helped. Even though someone set off a CS canister in the audience, The Stone Roses could not be derailed. It is not recorded whether they were carrying lemons in their pockets.

The Stone Roses returned to Manchester and prepared to release their next single. On November 1, 1989, they put out "Fool's Gold," which appeared on the US and subsequent UK versions of *The Stone Roses*. It would prove to be the band's most enduring song—the videogame company EA Sports used the song as the soundtrack in the 2004 edition of their FIFA (Federation of International Football Associations) soccer game. "Fool's Gold" showed the band at the peak of their powers. The languorous funk guitar made the single a great dance track, and for many it is the musical high point of The Stone Roses' career.

The band had yet to play a really big gig in London. But on November 18, they planned to play Alexandra Palace—affectionately known as Ally Pally—in north London. Although it had a capacity of 7,000, the venue was far from ideal.

"Originally we wanted play somewhere different," said Ian Brown. "So we tried to get a warehouse, but with all the parties involved it would have been difficult, and this was the only place that we could find that wasn't a rock 'n' roll gaff. The best legal alternative."

When the band arrived and did their sound-check, everything seem to be fine. But when the auditorium was filled with an overly boisterous audience, the hall's acoustics changed disastrously. That night they failed to set the capital alight.

"It wasn't crap," said Brown. "It was under par. We were struggling all night against the sound, as everyone knows. There were a lot of nothing moments but there were a lot of good moments too!"

This appraisal of the Alexandra Palace gig was not shared by all the members of the band.

"It was crap," said Mani. "It was a disaster."

Although this lackluster performance did bring The Stone Roses more recognition in London, their failure would be compounded three nights later when they appeared on BBC Two's flagship culture program, *The Late Show*.

The Roses were introduced to a national audience by the show's host Tracey MacLeod, who announced: "Last week a relatively unknown band sold out London's Alexandra Palace."

Up until this TV appearance, they had feigned a very anti-London attitude.

"It was a secret Manc thing," said Mani, "and we made the industry and everyone in it jump through our hoops. We never came down and went: 'Can I suck your cock and get a record deal, please?' Anyway, in the end we thought we'd go on a high-brow BBC Two program and play our music."

They were supposed to close the show with a live performance of "Made Of Stone," but disaster struck. They managed to overload the TV studio limiters and 60 seconds into the song, just as they hit the first chorus, their amps blew.

"We cranked up the guitars and blew all the fuses," said Ian Brown. "The needles must have gone straight to red and they didn't know how to handle that."

Brown lost his temper. He began upbraiding Tracey MacLeod, before storming off.

Those who saw the performance concluded that its sudden termination was no bad thing. They were not on form that night. Richard Luck, author of *The Madchester Scene*, said: "The band seemed to be playing at 33rpm and Brown sounded like a goose farting in the fog."

The power failure garnered them a great deal more press coverage, especially as Brown's reaction was to complain: "We're wasting our time lads," then bellow "Amateurs!" in the background while MacLeod tried to introduce the next item.

Even so, the BBC wanted the band to stay on so they could slot them in later in the show, if they could overcome the technical difficulties.

"Even after it all blew up," said Mani, "they said to us, 'Would you mind sticking around to the end? I'm sure we can sort everything out.' We were like 'bugger that' and so off we went."

The Stone Roses gained more notoriety from this as Brown's behavior attracted a lot of attention from the national media. It also got the band banned from the BBC. However they were already scheduled to play on the BBC TV's *Top Of The Pops* on November 23, with The Happy Mondays. The performance was allowed to go ahead, but after that they were rarely seen on British TV again.

Early the following year, they paid their infamous visit to Paul Birch (see British Graffiti).

"We did a lot of damage and they took us to court and that's when it hit us that we'd done a pretty bad thing," said Squire. "Mani was making jokes about us getting raped in prison."

In court, they pleaded guilty to criminal damage and were fined £3,600 ($5,400) each.

"The judge could have sent us to prison," said John Squire, "but he said in summing up that he wouldn't give us a custodial sentence because it could have enhanced our career, so we got off lightly."

The Stone Roses spent the early part of 1990 doing more tour dates in Scandinavia. They tried to arrange a small tour in the US, but the dates were canceled. Instead the band put their own money into a music festival on Spike Island near Widnes where they would headline. They wanted it to be a huge event, but the results were disappointing.

The Stone Roses album only went to number 86 in the US, but stayed in the album charts 26 weeks. In the UK, it went to number 19 and stayed in the charts for 86 weeks. This attracted the attention of David Geffen in Los Angeles, who reportedly paid them $6,000,000 to record their second album. However, the Geffen deal sidelined Gareth Evans, who began legal action against the band. This prevented The Stone Roses getting paid their substantial royalties on *The Stone Roses* album for years to come. Legal fees mounted and when they were eventually paid, the sums involved were no longer substantial.

The Stone Roses then spent four years recording their second album, aptly titled *The Second Coming*. It was during this time that the band began to fall apart, due to drugs and creative differences. When the album was released in 1995, Reni jumped ship. He was replaced with Robbie Maddix from London pop-rap band Rebel MC, and 1995 was a good touring year for The Stone Roses. Although *The Second Coming* was also doing good business, without Reni, the band slowly lost its cohesion.

They did a few more dates in Europe, and finally toured the US. Then John Squire broke his collar bone after a bicycle-riding accident. Consequently, a tour of Japan and an appearance at the prestigious Glastonbury Festival were canceled. When Squire recovered he played the year out with The Stone Roses, touring Japan, Australia, and the UK once more. After this, he left to form his own band, The Seahorses. Squire was replaced by Aziz Ibrahim, an old college friend of Ian Brown's. But with the two most talented members of the band now gone, The Stone Roses juddered to a halt in the summer of 1996, leaving behind them one of the classic pop albums of all time—*The Stone Roses*.

The Stone Roses is still considered as one of the greatest records of all time and consistently ranks in the top five in respected music polls. Its influence is still heard in the music of Oasis, Coldplay, and Kings Of Leon. It is seen as one of the defining records of the 1980s and its appeal seems set to last.

the song titles

"I Wanna Be Adored"

The album opens with "I Wanna Be Adored," the song they continued to open their gigs with. A superbly crafted pop anthem, it begins with a deep pounding bass line from Mani, while Reni's drums slowly build up in the background. Then Squire's guitar bursts into life sounding sweet and sharp. Brown's half-sung, almost choral voice echoes at the center of the music.

"She Bangs The Drums"

This track is a psychedelic tune with the guitar sound looming large. The sound of the track was compared to the Monkees when reviewed in the *NME*. On the surface it is a pure pop song, all light and innocence. However, the structure of the song is far more complex than anything the Monkees ever recorded, and Brown's lyrics are more hard-boiled, for example: "Kiss me where the sun don't shine/The past was yours but the future's mine." When it was released later that year as a single it gave The Stone Roses their first Top 40 hit in UK.

"'She Bangs The Drums' is about those brief moments when everything comes together," Squire explained. "Like staying up till dawn and watching the sun rise with somebody you love. And then regretting it bitterly."

"Waterfall"

Next on the album comes a near-perfect pop song, "Waterfall," with a jangling guitar harmony. Squire's guitar playing reaches its peak on this track and he demonstrates his mastery of the wah-wah pedal, which he was said to have reintroduced to British guitar music. Brown's vocals wash over the song and Reni adds to this effect with some backing vocals. The muffled lyrics seem to flow through the verses giving the track a druggie feel, before coming into focus in the choruses.

"The song is about a girl who sees all the bullshit, drops a [LSD] trip and goes to Dover," said Brown. "She tripping, she's about to get on this boat and she feels free."

"Don't Stop"
This song is generally considered to be the finest of the reverse tracks, which The Stone Roses habitually put on all their releases.

"Bye Bye Badman"
A light, breezy pop tune that sounds like a love song, "Bye Bye Badman," is in fact a song with an underlying political message.

As Brown explained: "If you go home and listen to 'Bye Bye Badman' and then imagine it's someone singing to a riot policeman in the barricades in Paris '68 you'll get a picture of what we're about. The song is a call to insurrection."

In an interview for Q magazine, Squire said that he had got the idea after he and Brown had watched a TV documentary about the 1968 Paris riots.

Despite the lyrical content of "Bye Bye Badman," The Stone Roses were never a truly political band, although they would occasionally touch upon social and political issues in their music. Usually, when they did this, they did it subtly. But not always.

"Elizabeth My Dear"

This cover of "Scarborough Fair" deals with the deposing and death of England's queen. The song runs for just under a minute and contains the lines: "Tear me apart and boil my bones/I'll not rest until she lost her throne/My aim is true my message is clear/It's curtains for you Elizabeth my dear." The Stone Roses may not have been particularly political, but they were still punks at heart. The anti-monarchy sentiments displayed here obviously refer back to the Sex Pistols' "God Save The Queen."

"(Song For My) Sugar Spun Sister"

Next comes one of the less inspiring songs on the album. "(Song For My) Sugar Spun Sister" is one of the older songs, which written back in 1986, and it lacks the clarity of vision displayed in the other, newer tracks. Although it is not a bad song, by necessity it gets overshadowed by the quality of the other tracks on the album.

"Made Of Stone"

Fortunately "Made Of Stone" follows "(Song For My) Sugar Spun Sister", so after a brief stumble the album becomes sure-footed again. "Made Of Stone" is a powerful pop anthem, hopeful and tragic at the same time. It shows the raw power of The Stone Roses' music in a way that few of the other tracks can match.

"Shoot You Down"

On this track, once again, Squire's guitar is bathed in wah-wah effects. "Shoot You Down" is funky and soulful, and is probably the main source of the comparison between John Squire and Jimi Hendrix. The tune is bouncy and fun, but again Brown's lyrics have hint of darkness to them. The Stone Roses once again juxtaposed light and dark in their music. This contradiction is a theme of the whole album.

"This Is The One"

The penultimate track, is the oldest song on the album. "This Is The One" was written in 1985 and served as The Stone Roses' anthem song before Brown and Squire came up with "Made Of Stone." It is a much more energetic offering with a well-crafted riff building up to a powerful crescendo. Even though this is an old song, it fits in with The Stone Roses' new material much better than "Sugar Spun Sister."

"I Am The Resurrection"

The album ends with "I Am The Resurrection," one of The Stone Roses' greatest songs. It is an epic pop work, running at eight minutes and twelve seconds.

"It was me who coaxed them to do that ending on '… Resurrection'," said Brown. "Only prog-rock groups and players up their own arses did ten-minute guitar solos. But I kept saying to them, 'Look, you're great. Let's do a ten-minute song where you're just playing and playing.' For two days I watched them work out the ending to that song. It was just fantastic and it still sounds amazing."

"I Am The Resurrection" does not only round off the album, but it would be the song that The Stone Roses would play to close their live performances until the end of their career. It showcases, in turn, John Squire's brilliant guitar work, Reni's drumming, Mani's powerful and steady work on the bass, and Ian Brown's singing, which ties the whole thing together. In many ways, it is the entire album encapsulated.

Postscript

Ian Brown is the only member of The Stone Roses to have a continuing career in the music business. In 1996, after 12 months locked away learning various musical instruments, Brown released his first solo album, *Unfinished Monkey Business*. And in January 1998, his first solo single "My Star" reached number five in the UK charts. Two more singles from *Unfinished Monkey Business*, "Corpses" and "Can't See Me," both attained some success. The album went gold and between the second and third singles, Brown launched his first solo tour of the UK and Europe. He toured continually through 1999.

In October 1999, the first single from *Golden Greats*, "Love Like A Fountain" was released. The album *Golden Greats* was released in November to massive critical acclaim and a further two singles were released in 2000, "Dolphins Were Monkeys" and "Golden Gaze". During that year Brown performed live in the UK, Europe, the US and Japan all through the year.

In 2001, Brown returned to the studio and produced his third album, *Music Of The Spheres*. He went on tour in the summer, and released the first single from the album, "F.E.A.R." in September, just ahead of the album's release. Increasingly he worked on collaborating with other bands and in 2004 he was back on the front cover of *NME* magazine.

appendix 1
the stone roses live

1984

October 23: Hampstead Moonlight Club, London, England
November 21: Labour Club, Exeter, England
November 22: Ad Lib Club, Kensington, London, England

1985

January 4: The Greyhound, Fulham, London, England
January 13: Piccadilly Radio Session, Manchester, England
January 19: The Marquee, London, England
February 8: Dingwalls, London, England
March 29: Clouds, Preston, England
April 10: Linköping, Sweden
April 11: Norrköping, Sweden
April 23: Lilla Marquee, Stockholm, Sweden
April 25: Stockholm, Sweden
April 30: Lidingö Stadium, Stockholm, Sweden
May 10: The International One, Manchester, England
(supporting It's Immaterial)
May 24: The Gallery, Manchester, England (supporting
Lavolta Lakota)
July 4: The Underground, Croydon, England (supporting
Doctor and The Medics)
July 20: Warehouse Party One, Manchester, England
(headlining)

August 2: The Marquee Club, London, England
August 27: The Hacienda, Manchester, England (supporting Playne Jayne)
September 11: Embassy Club, London, England (supporting Chiefs Of Relief)
October 26: The Riverside, London, England (supporting That Petrol Emotion)
November 22: Manchester University, Manchester, England
November 28: King George's Hall, Blackburn, England
November 30: Warehouse Party Two, Manchester, England

1986
March 5: King George's Hall, Blackburn, England
March 10: Manchester University, Manchester, England
March 25: Warwick University, Coventry, England
June 5: McGonagles, Dublin, Ireland

Andy Couzens leaves. Not replaced.

June: The Warehouse, Leeds, England
June: The Three Crows, London, England
July: The Ritz, Manchester, England
August: Mardis Gras, Liverpool, England

1987
January 30: The International One, Manchester, England
June 26: The International One, Manchester, England
July: Take Two, Sheffield, England
July: Planet X, Liverpool, England

August 11: Larks In The Park, Sefton Park, Liverpool,
England

Pete Garner leaves. Replaced by Mani.

November 13: The International One, Manchester, England

1988
November 26: Citadel, St Helens, England
November 29: Olives, Chester, England
December 11: The Venue, Edinburgh, Scotland

1989
February 17: Legends, Warrington, England
February 20: Sheffield University, Sheffield, England
February 23: Middlesex Polytechnic, England
February 27: Hacienda, Manchester, England
February 28: Escape Club, Brighton, England
March 1: Club Rio, Bradford, England
March 2: The Venue, Cardiff, Wales
March 3: JB's, Dudley, England
April 28: South Parade Pier, Portsmouth, England
April 29: Brunel University, Uxbridge, Middlesex, England
May 4: Liverpool Polytechnic, England
May 5: Queen's Hall, Widnes, England
May 6: International Two, Manchester, England
May 7: Sheffield University, Sheffield, England
May 8: Warehouse, Leeds, England
May 11: Trent Polytechnic, Nottingham, England
May 12: JBs, Dudley, England

May 13: Angel Centre, Tonbridge, England

May 15: ICA, London, England

May 17: Edwards No 8, Birmingham, England

May 19: Aberystwyth University, Aberystwyth, Wales

May 22: Dingwalls, Camden, London, England

May 24: Oxford Polytechnic, Oxford, England

May 25: Fridge, Shrewsbury, England

May 26: Elektra, Milton Keynes, England (Canceled due to recording)

May 27: Citadel, St Helens, England (Canceled due to recording)

May 30: Guildhall Foyer, Preston, England

June 3: Junction 10, Walsall, England

June 6: Majestic, Reading, England

June 7: Leicester University, Leicester, England

June 8: Lancaster University, Lancaster, England

June 2: Riverside, Newcastle, England

June 21: Venue, Edinburgh, Scotland

June 22: Rooftops, Glasgow, Scotland

June 23: Town Hall, Middlesbrough, England

June 24: Roadmenders, Northampton, England

June 25: Norwich Arts Centre, Norwich, England

June 26: Bierkeller, Bristol, England

June 27: Stratford-on-Avon Civic Hall, Stratford-on-Avon, England

June 28: Irish Centre, Birmingham, England

July 27: Riverside, Newcastle, England

August 12: Empress Ballroom, Blackpool, England

October 11: Amsterdam, Holland

October 12: Les Inrockuptibles Festival, Paris, France

November 18: Alexander Palace, London, England
November 21: *The Late Show*, BBC2, TV, London, England
November 23: *Top Of The Pops*, BBC1, TV, London, England

1990

May 15: Copenhagen, Denmark

May 16: Lund, Sweden

May 19: Oslo, Norway

May 27: Spike Island, near Widnes, England

June 7: Maysfield Leisure Centre, Belfast, Northern Ireland

June 9: Glasgow Green, Glasgow, Scotland

June ?: Feria De Nimes Festival, Spain (Canceled)

June 21: Chicago, Illinois, USA (Canceled)

June 22: New York City, New York, USA (Canceled)

June 29: Hollywood High School Gymnasium, California,
   USA (Canceled)

June 30: San Francisco, California, USA (Canceled)

1995

Reni leaves the band. Replaced by Robbie Maddix

April 19: Oslo, Norway

April 20: Stockholm, Sweden

April 26: Melkweg, Amsterdam, The Netherlands

April 27: La Luna, Brussels, Belgium

April 29: Cologne, Germany

May 1: Zurich, Switzerland

May 5: Le Bikini, Toulouse, France

May 7: Madrid, Spain

May 11: Elysee Montmartre, Paris, France

May 14: Atlanta, Georgia, USA

May 17: Washington DC, USA

May 18: Toronto, Canada

May 20: Manhattan Center Ballroom, New York City, USA

May 21: Boston, Massachusetts, USA

May 22: Webster Hall, New York City, USA

May 23: *David Letterman Show* (Canceled)

May 24: Philadelphia, Pennsylvania, USA

May 26: Riverport Amphitheatre, St Louis, Missouri, USA
(Pointfest 3)

May 27: Chicago, Illinois, USA

May 29: Los Angeles, California, USA

May 31: San Francisco, California, USA

June 5: Factory Hall, Sapporo, Japan (Canceled)

June 7: Club Citta', Kawasaki, Japan (Canceled)

June 8: Club Citta', Kawasaki, Japan (Canceled)

June 10: Century Hall, Nagoya, Japan (Canceled)

June 12: Nippon Budokan, Tokyo, Japan (Canceled)

June 13: Nippon Budokan, Tokyo, Japan (Canceled)

June 14: Kousei Nenkin Kaikan, Osaka, Japan (Canceled)

June 16: Yubin Chokin Hall, Hiroshima, Japan (Canceled)

June 17: Sun Palace Hall, Fukuoka, Japan (Canceled)

June 19: Festival Hall, Osaka, Japan (Canceled)

June 24: Glastonbury Festival, Glastonbury, England
(Canceled)

July 30: Stockholm, Sweden

July 31: Tampere, Finland

August 1: Helsinki, Finland

August 2: Helsinki, Finland

August 6: Cork, Ireland (Feile Festival)

September 11: Club Citta', Kawasaki, Japan

September 12: Nippon Budokan, Tokyo, Japan

September 13: Nippon Budokan, Tokyo, Japan

September 15: Convention Theater, Okinawa, Japan

September 17: IMP Hall, Osaka, Japan

September 18: Century Hall, Nagoya, Japan

September 20: Yubin Chokin Hall, Hiroshima, Japan

September 21: Sun Palace Hall, Fukuoka, Japan

September 24: IMP Hall, Osaka, Japan

September 25: IMP Hall, Osaka, Japan

September 27: Factory Hall, Sapporo, Japan

September 28: Club Citta', Kawasaki, Japan

October 1: Festival Hall, Brisbane, Australia

October 2: The Enmore Theatre, Sydney, Australia

October 3: The Enmore Theatre, Sydney, Australia

October 5: The Metro, Melbourne, Australia

October 7: The Thebarton Theatre, Adelaide, Australia

October 8: The Metropolis, Perth, Australia

October 9: The Metropolis, Perth, Australia

November 28: Spa Theatre, Bridlington, England

November 30: Civic Hall, Wolverhampton, England

December 1: Corn Exchange, Cambridge, England

December 2: Brighton Centre, Brighton, England

December 4: Newport Centre, Newport, Wales

December 5: Exeter University, Exeter, England

December 7: De Montford Hall, Leicester, England

December 8: Brixton Academy, London, England

December 9: Brixton Academy, London, England

December 11: Rivermead, Reading, England

December 12: University of East Anglia, Norwich, England

December 13: Town and Country, Leeds, England

December 15: Royal Court, Liverpool, England

December 16: Ice Rink, Whitley Bay, England

December 17: Aberdeen Music Hall, Aberdeen, Scotland

December 19: Barrowlands, Glasgow, Scotland

December 20: Barrowlands, Glasgow, Scotland

December 22: Apollo Manchester, Manchester, England

December 23: Apollo Manchester, Manchester, England

December 27: Sheffield Arena, Sheffield, England

December 29: Wembley Arena, London, England

John Squire leaves the band. Replaced by Aziz Ibrahim.

1996

August 2: Festival Internacional, Benicassim, Spain

August 10: Festival Vilar de Mouros, Portugal

August 11: Skanderborg Festival, Denmark

August 23: Lowlands Festival, Netherlands

August 25: Reading Festival, Reading, England

appendix 2
discography

September 1985, So Young/Tell Me (Thin Line LINE 001, 12-inch)

May 1987, Sally Cinnamon/Here It Comes/All Across The Sand (Revolver/Black 12REV 36, 12-inch)

October 1988, Elephant Stone/The Hardest Thing In The World (Silvertone ORE 1, 7-inch)

October 1988, Elephant Stone (7-inch version)/Full Fathom Five/The Hardest Thing In The World (Silvertone ORET 1, 12-inch)

February 1989, Sally Cinnamon/Here It Comes/All Across The Sand (Revolver/Black 12REV 36, 12-inch reissue, different versions of Sally Cinnamon and All Across The Sand)

February 1989, Made Of Stone/Going Down (Silvertone ORE 2, 7-inch)

February 1989, Made Of Stone/Going Down/Guernica (Silvertone ORE 2T, 12-inch)

April 1989, THE STONE ROSES—I Wanna Be
Adored/She Bangs The Drums/ Waterfall/Don't Stop/Bye
Bye Badman/Elizabeth My Dear/(Song For My) Sugar Spun
Sister/Made Of Stone/Shoot You Down/This Is The One/I
Am The Resurrection (Silvertone ORE LP 502, LP)
(Silvertone ORE CD 502, CD)
Subsequent reissues contained other bonus tracks.

July 1989, She Bangs The Drums/Standing Here (Silvertone
ORE 6, 7-inch)

July 1989, She Bangs The Drums/Mersey Paradise/Standing
Here (Silvertone ORET 6, 12-inch)

July 1989, She Bangs The Drums/Mersey Paradise/Standing
Here/Simone (Silvertone ORECD 6, CD)

July 1989, She Bangs The Drums/Mersey Paradise/Standing
Here/Simone (Silvertone OREC 6, cassette)

November 1989, What The World Is Waiting For/Fools
Gold 4.15 (Silvertone ORE 13, 7-inch)

November 1989, Fools Gold 4.15/What The World Is
Waiting For (Silvertone ORE 13, 7-inch repressing with
titles reversed)

November 1989, What The World Is Waiting For/Fools
Gold 9.35 (Silvertone ORET 13, 12-inch)

November 1989, Fools Gold 9.35/What The World Is
Waiting For/Fools Gold 4.15 (Silvertone ORET 13, 12-inch
repressing with titles reversed)

November 1989, Fools Gold 9.35/What The World Is
Waiting For/Fools Gold 4.15 (Silvertone ORECD 13, CD)

November 1989, Fools Gold 9.35/What The World Is
Waiting For/Fools Gold 4.15 (Silvertone OREC 13,
cassette)

December 1989, Sally Cinnamon/Here It Comes
(Revolver/Black REV 36, 7-inch)

December 1989, Sally Cinnamon (7-inch single mix)/Sally
Cinnamon (12-inch single mix)/Here It Comes/All Across
The Sand (Revolver/Black REV XD36, CD)

December 1989, Sally Cinnamon (7-inch single mix)/Sally
Cinnamon (12-inch single mix)/Here It Comes/All Across
The Sand (Revolver/Black REV MC 36, cassette)

January 1990, Sally Cinnamon (7-inch single mix)/Sally
Cinnamon (12-inch single mix)/Here It Comes/All Across
The Sand (Revolver/Black REV XD36, CD reissued twice in
January 1990)

January 1990, Fools Gold (The Top Won mix)/Fools Gold
(The Bottom Won mix) (Silvertone ORECD13, Gold CD)

February 1990, Elephant Stone/Full Fathom Five/The Hardest Thing In The World/Elephant Stone (7-inch version) (Silvertone ORECD 1, CD)

February 1990, Elephant Stone/Full Fathom Five/The Hardest Thing In The World/Elephant Stone (7-inch version) (Silvertone OREC 1, cassette)

March 1990, Made Of Stone/Going Down/Guernica (Silvertone ORECD2, CD)

March 1990, Made Of Stone/Going Down/Guernica (Silvertone OREC 2, cassette)

July 1990, One Love/Something's Burning (Silvertone ORE 17, 7-inch)

July 1990, One Love/Something's Burning (Silvertone ORET 17, 12-inch)

July 1990, One Love (Paul Schroeder mix/Something's Burning (Silvertone OREZ 17, 12-inch)

July 1990, One Love/Something's Burning (Silvertone ORECD 17, CD)

September 1991, I Wanna Be Adored/Where Angels Play (Silvertone ORE 31, 7-inch)

September 1991, I Wanna Be Adored/Where Angels Play/Sally Cinnamon (Live At The Hacienda) (Silvertone OREZ 31, 12-inch with color print) (Silvertone ORET 31, 12-inch without)

September 1991, I Wanna Be Adored/Where Angels Play/I Wanna Be Adored (Live At The Hacienda)/Sally Cinnamon (Live At The Hacienda) (Silvertone ORECD 31, CD)

January 1992, Waterfall (7-inch version)/One Love (7-inch version) (Silvertone ORE 35, 7-inch)

January 1992, Waterfall (12-inch version)/One Love (Adrian Sherwood mix) (Silvertone OREZT 35, 12-inch)

January 1992, Waterfall (7-inch version)/One Love (7-inch version)/Waterfall (12-inch version)/One Love (12-inch version) (Silvertone ORECD 35, CD)

January 1992, Waterfall (7-inch version)/One Love (7-inch version) (Silvertone OREC 35, cassette)

April 1992, I Am The Resurrection (Pan and Scan Radio version)/I Am The Resurrection (Highly Resurrected Dub) (Silvertone ORE 40, 7-inch)

April 1992, I Am The Resurrection (Pan and Scan Radio version)/I Am The Resurrection (Highly Resurrected Dub) (Silvertone OREC 40, cassette)

April 1992, I Am The Resurrection (Extended Radio Club mix)/I Am The Resurrection (Stoned Out Club mix)/I Am The Resurrection (LP version)/Fools Gold (The Bottom Won mix) (Silvertone ORECD 40, CD)

index